AF269214

THE CELESTINE PROPHECY FULFILLED

THE INSIGHT OF NO FREE WILL

NICK VALE

Author's Tranquility Press
ATLANTA, GEORGIA

Copyright © 2025 by NICK VALE

All rights reserved. No part of this publication may be reproduced, distributed or transmitted in any form or by any means, including photocopying, recording, or other electronic or mechanical methods, without the prior written permission of the publisher, except in the case of brief quotations embodied in critical reviews and certain other noncommercial uses permitted by copyright law. For permission requests, write to the publisher, addressed "Attention: Permissions Coordinator," at the address below.

NICK VALE/Author's Tranquility Press
3900 N Commerce Dr. Suite 300 #1255
Atlanta, GA 30344
www.authorstranquilitypress.com

Ordering Information:
Quantity sales. Special discounts are available on quantity purchases by corporations, associations, and others. For details, contact the "Special Sales Department" at the address above.

The Celestine Prophecy Fulfilled: The Insight of No Free Will/Nick Vale
Paperback: 978-1-966088-29-5
eBook: 978-1-966088-31-8

Contents

This Book is Dedicated to and for:

Religious and Spiritual leaders who live in an echo chamber of wishful thinking and motivated reasoning that have bamboozled and bullied people into believing that "God gave man free will" is an unchallengeable assumption.

Why is that? The following always seems to ring true:

"It Is Difficult to Get a Man to Understand Something When His Salary Depends Upon His Not Understanding It."

— Upton Sinclair

"New truth is often uncomfortable. This is especially true for the holders of power the new truth threatens. New truth is often looked at as blasphemy."

— Nick Vale

This Book is also Dedicated to and for:

Future generations who will understand man's will is not free, Henry Thoreau, James Redfield, and The Law of Parsimony/Occam's Razor:

"Rather than love, than money, than fame, give me truth."

— Henry Thoreau

"In this awareness, we can release our own pattern of controlling, and discover a specific truth, a mission, we are here to share that helps evolve humanity toward this new level of reality."

— James Redfield, The Celestine Prophecy

The Law of Parsimony/Occam's Razor

1. *If determinism is true, then there is no free will.*
2. *If indeterminism is true, then there is no free will.*
3. *Either determinism is true, or indeterminism is true.*
4. *Therefore, there is no free will (from 1-3)*

Before We Begin…What does the term "Free Will" mean to you? What is your definition of it? Do you believe you have "free will?"

After three plus decades of waiting, The Celestine Prophecy has finally been fulfilled. The 1993 legendary and influential Prophecy predicted that an emerging culture and spiritual awakening unlike human beings had ever experienced before was about to occur. The Prophecy boldly foresaw that human beings would be able to achieve a huge breakthrough in spiritual consciousness. The wait is finally over as the long sought-after breakthrough and hence fulfillment of The Celestine Prophecy has now been attained. What is it? HUMAN BEINGS DO NOT HAVE FREE WILL. The implications of this bombshell breakthrough are truly historical. The first domino to fall (step) will be the declaration that the nonsensical free will age become a relic of the past and be pronounced dead. The next step will be the truthful resurrection of humanity as we all step into and see the light of a brand new "no free will" awareness and reality. The fourteen insights and revelations contained in the completion of these two steps are the fulfillment of The Celestine Prophecy. The No Free Will Insight will be for the betterment of mankind and change the world forever. With free will no longer in play, a tremendous leap in the understanding of reality will occur elevating us to live in total and complete harmony with nature and the laws of the universe. The Holy Grail of Insights is that free will is an illusion and doesn't exist. This insight contains many far-reaching and life altering realizations and transforms just about every facet of the human condition. For example, society will soon have to learn and then accept the new truth that Heaven and Hell cannot exist without free will because deep fundamental blame or praise (final judgment) and subsequent eternal damnation or salvation will no longer be possible. With the illusory free will bubble out of the way and bursted, the no free will truth will be able to reach a critical mass. It will be at this point that the "Thou Shall Not Fundamentally Praise or Blame" consciousness will earn its wings and begin to ascend. During this ascension, humanity will victoriously rise from the ashes of the very harmful and destructive free will age and then bear witness to the birth of the no free will consciousness epoch. A far more compassionate, truer and fairer humanity with far less severe punishment, vengeance and retribution will then be upon us.

Ok now let's get to it:

There are only two ways in which you can do something:

#1 Is Because you are forced to do it.
#2 Is Because you want to do it.

Now obviously #1 is not free will because you are being forced. So, this entire book is about how #2 is also not free will. Just because you "want" to do something does not grant free will as we do not get to choose or control what we want to do in the first place. Wants and desires come from background causes of which we are not in control of and not the "free" choosers of. We are simply lucky to have moral desires and unlucky to have immoral desires. Yes, we can choose our wants and desires, but we do not get to choose <u>*WHAT*</u> those desires and wants are in the first place. If we could, who amongst us would choose to be depressed, evil, or a life of crime?

"Free will is an illusion. Our wills are simply not of our own making. Thoughts and intentions emerge from background causes of which we are unaware and over which we exert no conscious control. We do not have the freedom we think we have."

— Sam Harris, *Free Will*

As many of us know the book "The Celestine Prophecy" published in 1993 was a book that contained many spiritual insights. It also contained The Prophecy that humanity was about to learn the TRUTH about how human lives are lived and how a huge spiritual breakthrough was about to occur.

Well, here we are so many years later – The fulfillment of The Celestine Prophecy and THE INSIGHT OF ALL INSIGHTS is now upon us. The Insight is this: The Insight of There's No Free Will. The Celestine Prophecy is now Hereby Fulfilled!

The consciousness of Humanity is Hereby Raised!

As per the Celestine Prophecy's guiding principle – The Insight of No Free Will was discovered via paying very close attention to numerous magical, mystical, and meaningful coincidences which got me to read the Celestine Prophecy in the first place and to discover that the No Free Will Insight had been left out. I simply followed the synchronistic energy path presented to me that gave me the energy and attention span needed to write this book you are reading now. It appears that James Redfield may have understood how and why free will is impossible, but in The Celestine Prophecy he never just comes out and directly says it.

Here below is as close as he got to saying it:

"We finally concluded that everything that occurs in nature does so according to some natural law, that each event has a direct physical and understandable cause."

— James Redfield, *The Celestine Prophecy*

The declaration that human beings do not have free will is not directly mentioned in the original 1993 Celestine Prophecy or in its subsequent additional insights or 2006 movie of the same name. Here is one of my main motivations for writing this book:

"Once you learn what life is about, there is no way to erase the knowledge. If you try to do something else with your life, you will always sense that you are missing something. The truth you are pursuing is as important as the evolution of the universe itself, for it enables evolution to continue."

— James Redfield, *The Celestine Prophecy*

For as long as I can remember, I was told "it's your choice." But is it? The answer may surprise you. Do humans have free will?

"You see, the problem in life isn't receiving answers. The problem is in identifying your current questions. Once you get the questions right, the answers always come."

— James Redfield, *The Celestine Prophecy*

Foreword - Part One

In The Beginning . . .

The 1993 Celestine Prophecy taught us that a huge spiritual awakening and discovery was about to occur. The discovery that human beings do not have free will is that discovery. The Prophecy has now come true and has been fulfilled with the Insight that human beings do not have free will:

The #1 reason why people believe in free will is because they want it to be true. Wanting something to be true does not make it true. The present-day free will paradigm/belief is currently stuck in the motivated reasoning/wishful thinking echo chamber of religion. There can be no epiphany to the contrary in religion because they (religious and spiritual leaders) have too much invested in free will being real. Religious people simply enjoy their belief in free will far too much and as Jack Nicholson said in A Few Good Men "You can't handle the Truth!" It is mostly because of the deeply ingrained religious belief that free will is real that the vast majority of people on planet earth do in fact believe in free will. Then peer pressure. People believe in free will because conformity and feeling "normal" is a form of pleasure. People have no choice but to always go towards pleasure and away from pain (what gives them the most overall life satisfaction). People who believe in the nonsense of free will reflect this psychological law. Now it's time for a change… When "do this—to get that" no longer works, you will need a new belief system to accommodate that reality. People are always doing the very best they can at the time with the knowledge and data they had at the time. Law and Order (or morality) will not break down with the advent of the knowledge contained in this book. Actions still have consequences (with or without free will). Free will is not needed for actions to have consequences. Free will is false but consequences are real. We also do not need free will or God to be moral for that same exact reason. All we need is an agreed upon moral code made by human beings. We then need to be conditioned like everything else in life (rewarded when we act morally and punished when we don't). Once again and to be clear, actions will always still have consequences. We were taught that man's will is free. We were taught all wrong. We could not have done otherwise with who we were at the time, the knowledge we had at the time, and the way the entire state of the universe was at the time. First, I will briefly discuss and connect the first two original insights from the 1993 book The Celestine Prophecy: An Adventure by James Redfield to the work presented here. Then I will proceed with the Fourteen Insights/Chapters of this book. These new Insights/Chapters will fulfill THE PROPHECY foretold 32 years ago by explaining that the "new spiritual awakening" in the original book is this:

Humanity's consciousness has now evolved to a state in which everyone can understand that human beings do not have free will.

THE FIRST INSIGHT . . . A CRITICAL MASS

"A new spiritual awakening is occurring in human culture, an awakening brought about by a critical mass of individuals who experience their lives as a spiritual unfolding."

— James Redfield, *The Celestine Prophecy*

Once you fully internalize that there is no such thing as "free will" will you then understand that all of life is pre-determined and everything that happens on earth is God Willed/Higher Power Willed/Universe Willed. Mankind does not have any control of what happens on earth. We therefore have no choice but to experience our lives as a "spiritual unfolding" of which we are simply the spectators of. We simply have no choice but to always be doing the very best we can AT THE TIME with the knowledge we had at the time. We do not get to choose how intelligent we are, were, or will become. We do not get to choose our soul or spirit. We do not get to choose our nature or nurture. We do not get to choose our consciousness, intentions, thoughts, or desires. We must become "ready" for everything which includes reading this book. Emotional, mental, spiritual, physical, metaphysical, and psychological states all have a causal history to them (cause and effect). We all possess a personal causal history learning curve/chain of events (think of a long line of dominoes starting from the moment of our conception) which determines how/when we learn things and become ready for things. We cannot control when we become ready for things. We cannot control when we change our mind, beliefs, or perspective about something. Once again, we did not choose how intelligent we are or how logical or rational we are. We are not a failure if we fail at something because we do not have free will. If we could have done otherwise, rest assured, we would have done otherwise.

"Trading Places Theory" also refutes free will:

 How can there be "ultimate moral responsibility?"

Trading Places Theory: Say this to yourself . . .

"If I were an 'evil' other/another person, I'd be that 'evil' other/another person. Atom for Atom, Quark for Quark, Neuron for Neuron, Neutrino for Neutrino, Boson for Boson, and the same exact 'evil' mind and soul and all . . . I'd have that person's same exact consciousness. With his/her exact same genetics, his/her exact same conditioning (how he/she was raised), and his/her exact same 'evil' mind and soul. I'd be him/her in every exact and conceivable way and would've acted the same exact way in every regard possible. 'Free Will' is nowhere to be found."

Why do people continue to believe in "free will?"

They have an emotional/psychological attachment to it. They feel better believing in it than not believing in it. The opposite is also true. These people (free will believers) become psychologically, spiritually, and emotionally disturbed or unhinged by not believing in it ("free will"). Simply put, not believing in "free will" or often confused with just not having "freedom" greatly depresses them. People have no choice but to believe in free will because to do otherwise would inflict severe psychological, spiritual, and emotional damage upon themselves and in effect would shatter their entire life paradigm (world view). Everything is a conditioned response.

The people who believe in free will are conditioned to do so because they believe there is more pleasure in believing in it (free will) than not. We have no choice but to choose what we predict will yield us the most amount of overall life satisfaction available to us in every so called "free choice" decision we make. We also have no choice but to always be doing the very best we can at the time with the data and knowledge we had at the time to make the best decision for ourselves we could at the time. Free Will is a very harmful belief. It makes people believe that they are failures when they cannot succeed at something. We are not free to choose things that do not occur to us at the time. Society will soon have to learn something called "pragmatic blame" aka "pragmatic blameless responsibility" (see Insight/Chapter Two for much more on this concept). Man can self-cause nothing. Not even a single thought. Yes, you are pragmatically blamelessly/faultlessly responsible for your karma (cause and effect). But ultimately and fundamentally you are not responsible for your karma (cause and effect). Human beings are an overly egocentric species with an overly exaggerated and inflated false sense of self-importance and suffer from delusions of grandeur (as being able to be a first or self-causer like a little God). Human beings also have an insatiable need to find meaning through their personal accomplishments which they can't help but take full credit for. The need for control, validation/acknowledgment (look at me!

look at what I did!) and ego stroking/pleasing are some of the many reasons why human beings incorrectly believe in the magical quality of "free will." For humans to admit there is no free will, this would rob them of their highly cherished need for control and sense of self-worth/self-esteem (and justification for their high salaries).

Most humans find it much too psychologically painful to even discuss this issue as the mere idea that free will is an illusion would also mean the self is an illusion and that we are not so different in many ways to an inanimate object or an animal. Desperation for meaning as described above is one of the many reasons human beings incorrectly believe in free will. Once again, just because you want something to be true does not make it true.

THE SECOND INSIGHT . . . THE LONGER NOW

"This awakening represents the creation of a new, more complete worldview, which replaces a five-hundred-year-old preoccupation with secular survival and comfort."

— James Redfield, *The Celestine Prophecy*

The Celestine Prophecy predicted and foretold that we will soon see a new phase of human progress and that humanity is now awakening from a materialistic worldview. It predicts and foretells that we will soon evolve into a whole new human consciousness. *The insight that human beings do not have free will is the fulfillment of The Celestine Prophecy (prophesized thirty-two years ago). Understanding there is No Free Will allows for the next step for humanity to occur. This next step is to evolve humanity into a whole new consciousness. The bursting of the free will illusory bubble is for the betterment of mankind.* Human beings are just human computers/human robots/human puppets. The puppeteers are the programs or operating systems that we are running. They are # 1 – always having no choice but to seek more and more overall life satisfaction (the satisfaction imperative) and #2

– the optimization imperative (always doing the very best we can at the time with the data and knowledge we had/have at the time). This means we always have no choice but to do what we do, and we could not have done otherwise (with the knowledge we had at the time). When an accident or mistake occurs and we did everything in our power to avoid it, then it must be called fate. There is no other choice in the matter.

The last great truth to be discovered is that free will is false and is a grand illusion. We do not control our own destiny. We are just a witness to our own life.

Dear Reader,

Is someone forcing you or making you read this letter? If not, then you will say to me it is your free will to read this letter right now…. But… You are not using your free will to read this letter. You did not decide if you wanted to read this letter in the first place. The desire to read it just arose and you acted on it, but it (the desire to read this letter) was not under your conscious control to begin with. Yes, you can do what you desire to do but you cannot control or choose what those desires are in the first place. Put another way, reading this letter right now was predetermined by your causal sub/unconscious mind and/or by random quantum events and effects that were also not in your conscious control. Since most people have been conditioned to believe in free will, changing the world's point of view will be extremely hard. Our educational and mental health system need to be changed as soon as possible regarding this free will issue. I believe that deep down people always prefer the truth over lies and this leaves a window of hope. If people can become intrigued, they'll investigate, try to find the truth, and eventually come to the inevitable conclusion that free will is a lie. Please join me in this effort. Change is a causal process. Just because human beings do not have free will doesn't mean they cannot change. As soon as human beings internalize that there is more pleasure in not believing in free will than there is in believing in it, will they be ready for this change. In fact, change is what living in the universe is all about. People are constantly changing based on the stimuli they encounter in their lives. You can help someone change by clearly explaining to them the teachings of The Celestine Prophecy now being fulfilled (you become the new stimuli they encounter). Change = (Cause and Effect) x Time. One moment in time creates the next moment in time. Think of dominoes being moments in time and/or people knocking into one another in a long chain of dominoes. This is called the "domino effect." Each domino falling causes the next domino to fall so on and so forth. You can be the domino that helps another person change their mind and go from believing in free will to not believing in free will. Human beings are in and part of the cause-and-effect universe. Human beings cannot escape this simple concept of causality. Please help (be the domino) and change one person's mind about this free will issue.

Thank You, Nick Vale

Here is a simplified story/example of how a person can change without free will. In this story/example please notice how the "go with the flow" nature of seeking pleasure and avoiding pain creates change and how free will is not needed. All the actions in this story adhere to the law that human beings have no choice but to seek greater and greater overall life satisfaction and as per The Celestine Prophecy – how there is energy in coincidences that help guide us to do so.

There is no free will needed in this story below, yet the main character John's life changes dramatically (for the better).

John was down on his luck. He was very anxious and somewhat socially awkward. He was also lonely and depressed. He was living with his parents and was in his mid to late 20s. He could not find a job as none were available. One day his mother insisted he do an errand for her and go to the local mall. John's driver's license had recently been suspended because of a DUI so he had to take the bus to the mall. At the bus stop he wanted a cigarette but realized he had left them at home. At the bus stop he saw a girl who was smoking. He asked her if he could bum a cigarette off her and she said yes. The two began talking and continued to talk on the bus ride. He found out her name was Maria and she was very nice. On the bus he noticed some cars he liked out the window and pointed them out to Maria. He then told Maria about how much he loved cars and especially fixing his father's car. Maria took a liking to John and told him that just earlier that day her father was upset because one of his employees had quit his entry level Auto Shop position which was in his neighborhood. She suggested that he come to the Auto Shop later that day to speak with her father and see if he could work there. After he went to the mall, he took Maria's suggestion and went to her father's Auto Shop. At the Auto Shop John met Louis (Maria's father). Louis and John hit it off immediately as they both liked driving the exact same rare type of car. It turns out that it was the same exact model, brand and type John's father owned and the one that John enjoyed fixing all the time. Louis hired John. As time went on, John and Louis became good friends, and John grew confident in every single way. His newfound confidence also made him less socially awkward and less depressed. Maria started to find him attractive and believed in him. Now many years have gone by, and John and Maria are happily married with two children. Soon, Louis will retire, and John will be the owner. Louis will even change the name of his Auto Shop from Louis Auto Shop to Louis and Son Auto Shop. John is now living a much happier life and is so very grateful each day. Every day he thanks God for his wonderful wife and two beautiful children. He is truly grateful to God for how lucky he was to meet Maria that day at the bus stop.

Human decision making is never uncaused, and we are not first or self-causers.

The Celestine Prophecy Fulfilled: The Insight of No Free Will

Foreword - Part Two

In The Beginning . . .

Openly refuting "free will," will be the most important "taboo" subject matter ever discussed and debated in the history of time when it finally comes out of hiding. Enough with academia and philosophy class already. Let's bring this topic to the people (Main Street). The illusion of free will is so prevalent in our society that many people don't even know that they have been living a life of lies all these years. Believing in free will is the mythical monster of the times we currently live in. This book can prove and persuade you to the truth that free will doesn't exist. This book can also show you how a planet without free will is a better and more compassionate planet to live on. Make this promise to yourself before you begin: I am now going to look at the issue of "free will." Do we as human beings have the ability to make our own decisions in all matters of life? Is it left up to you and me to decide how our lives will be lived or is it left up to God (the entirety of the universe)? We either have "free will" or we don't. Many people love to say they have "a little free will." A "little free will" means you do in fact believe in free will. This is a black or white issue. You either have free will or you don't. The question is this: Is your life up to you? Or is it predetermined? Did everything have to turn out exactly as it did and will? Or could you have done otherwise and had your life turn out differently than it did? Are you in control of how your life will turn out going forward or is it predetermined? The vast majority of people currently believe in free will and a very tiny, small minority do not. So, who is correct? We cannot have two truths fighting against each other; if two truths do fight against each other then what you have is not truth. There can only be one truth in this matter and it's about time to understand that free will doesn't exist and is categorically and axiomatically impossible.

The Insight that there is no such thing as Free Will means that our lives are predetermined. Simply put, we live our lives according to our own personal causal chain learning curves and our unique personal causal histories (how we are conditioned by our personal cause and effect chain). We have no choice but to attempt to attain more and more overall life satisfaction (according to our own personal and unique perspectives). Sometimes when we attempt to attain something and plan what we feel is a "good idea/decision at the time" it backfires (our prediction was faulty) and we experience suffering. This does not nullify or disqualify the fact that we made the attempt to attain what was best for us in the first place. These are called life lessons, and we learn from them. Some people like to say that cause and effect doesn't apply to them because they are made of a non—material or non—physical spirit or soul.

Here are three possibilities of a non-physical entity within you:

#1 If there is a non-physical entity within you (soul or spirit), you are not in conscious control of it and you did not choose it in the first place (for example some of us have "good" souls and others have "evil" souls). Why would anyone freely choose an "evil" soul. <u>Free Will is not saved</u>.

#2 Even if your non-physical entity is just an advisor of yours (trying to push you in one direction or another or just a part of you), free will is not saved. Your "advisor" just becomes part of your causal chain (chain of causality in one moment in time) just like any other person would be. This soul or spirit interaction (the immaterial part of you interacting with your physical part of you) must happen in a moment in time thereby entering the physical world (space time continuum). One moment in time is the total and complete cause of the next moment in time. <u>Free Will is not saved</u>.

#3 If you claim you are your soul/spirit, and your soul/spirit is you and under your conscious control and therefore you are not a physical being whatsoever (and therefore no interaction between the immaterial you and material you are needed), then I would answer — <u>you are still existing in a moment in time.</u> One moment in time is the total and complete cause of the next moment in time and this includes the soulful, emotional, spiritual, psychological, mental, metaphysical, supernatural and any or all immaterial causation. In summary, it does not matter how things are caused (physical or non-physical). All that matters is that everything must have a cause and is caused (one moment in time causing the next moment in time). The linear arrow of moments in time (carries with it everything about you – physical and non-physical) and it points in one direction only. That direction is one moment in time is the total and complete cause of the next moment in time (past to present to future). <u>Free Will is not saved</u>.

Either way in summary:

Non-Physical causation (if you believe in such a thing) still must happen in a moment in time. Moments in time are linear as one moment in time *(the entire state of the universe and everything in it) is the total and complete cause of the next moment in time (the entire state of the universe and everything in it). So on and so forth. Conclusion: Free Will is not saved.

*The entire state of the universe includes all immaterial and numinous entities including ghosts, spirits and souls etc. (if you believe in such things).

The Celestine Prophecy Fulfilled: The Insight of No Free Will

The Definition of Free Will

Before we begin, I'm not going to insult your intelligence and start splitting hairs with semantics that attempt to differentiate between the different types of free will. To be quick and to summarize, there is no such thing as free will no matter how many versions of free will the experts proclaim there to be. Your life is not up to you/within your control. That's it right there. Full stop. There is a scheme out there to confuse you between such things as "libertarian free will" and "compatibilist free will." In case you didn't know – libertarian free will (the ability to have chosen and done otherwise with the rule that it must be the exact same starting conditions) is obviously false as you could not have done otherwise based on what your desire was at the time the so called "free choice" was made. Therefore, we can conclude, the only way you could have "freely chosen" and done otherwise at the exact same moment in time as the first time would be if you had a different consciousness/desire/brain state and therefore would have had to have been a completely different human being (meaning the same person but with a different desire/brain state/consciousness). This obviously violates the rule that for libertarian free will to exist, the starting conditions must be identical. Therefore, it is easy to conclude that libertarian free will is impossible. In short, you could only have done otherwise if you had wanted to do otherwise. But since you didn't want to do otherwise, you couldn't have done otherwise. This is because human beings cannot be **causa sui** (the cause of itself, self-caused) which leads to this next point.... It is cheating to say, "well I could have easily wanted something else." But you didn't want that "something else" option at the time because of who you were at the time and trying to change, twist, and contort the actual facts of your life (what you wanted at the time) in order to argue for why there is libertarian free will (or for that matter any kind of free will) will come across as being just plain silly to anyone who is logical (such as me for example). And now about so called "compatibilist free will" (meaning determinism and free will are compatible). This idea that free will and determinism are compatible is also totally illogical and obviously false. This is because.... a) free will is a completely made-up thing and is not compatible with anything (because it doesn't exist in the first place). And b) it is <u>especially not compatible with determinism</u> as the very word determinism literally means cause and effect (no free will). In no universe are free will and determinism compatible unless of course you change the definition of free will (which many people love to do) to mean something other than what it ACTUALLY MEANS which is.... Free will = YOUR LIFE IS UP TO YOU (not predetermined). Therefore, it is easy to conclude, free will (your life being up to you) and determinism (cause and effect) are not compatible no matter what guys like Dan Dennett believed. People who tell you that you have some type or version of free will (Deepak Chopra/all religious leaders/just about everyone on earth) are practicing indirect violence on you as they are blaming you for messing up (when you did/do/will). They believe that hard work, skill, and drive will make you and them a success. That may be true, but it's not guaranteed, and these traits/qualities/values cannot be freely chosen. It is not to your credit or your fault if you do or do not possess these qualities. It is not to your credit if you are not lazy and not to your fault if you are. Laziness, like hardworking, is a neurological condition that you are not in control of. The belief in free will makes people feel very badly about themselves amongst other negative things (keep reading) when they inevitably mess up. One more clarifying thing: When I say your life is determined (cause and effect) that also means the exact same thing as predetermined.

Ok let's begin......

Let me introduce you to what the term "free will" means.

The American Heritage College Dictionary:

"Free Will" *n.* 1. The ability or discretion to choose; free choice. 2. The power of making free choices that are unconstrained by external circumstances or by an agency such as fate or divine will.

*Meriam-Webster Collegiate Dictionary/*Eleventh Edition:

"Free Will" *n.* freedom of humans to make choices that are not determined by prior causes or by divine intervention.

It is useless to have a refutation of this term "free will" unless we define it first. As can be seen from our dictionaries, the term "free will" means the ability to make "free choices." Not just choices, but "free" choices. Notice that our dictionaries are specific in stating that it is "free choice" that is the definition of "free will," rather than just "choice" alone. To be an expression of "free will," choices must also be free.

Free from what? We just read it:

- Free from "prior causes."
- Free from "constraint."
- Free from "external circumstances."
- Free from "fate."
- Free from "divine will."
- Free from "divine intervention.

Those who argue for free will, however, refuse to be held to these precise and concise definitions. They want the mere ability to "make a choice" to be considered an act of "free will." Well, it is nothing of the kind. Making a choice has absolutely nothing to do with the doctrine of "free will." This is easily demonstrated. Computers make "choices." They can make millions of "choices" per second. It would take a million people to make that many choices in a second. All that these marvelous machines do is make choices. Now then, will anyone maintain that computers have unprogrammed and uncaused free wills? So now we have proof that making choices is not the same as "free will." Computers do not have "free wills," yet they can make choices, but those choices are anything but free. Their choices are all a matter of pre-programming. They cannot think and act independently of their "causes" otherwise known as their programming or inputs. Neither can man think or do anything outside of the realm of his or her "causes," "programming," or "inputs." For an effect to be present, there must first be a cause, and once something is caused, the effect must follow, and neither could have been prevented. There has not been one example ever created in the entire history of the entire universe that can be presented by any scientific method known to man (including such things as Heisenberg's Uncertainty Principle or the Double Slit Experiment) that can demonstrate that man's will is free from causality. Neither is there an example in all Scripture that can be shown to be the exercise of a will that is free from causality.

Ok let's switch gears here and move on:

What is the difference between a partial preference and a full preference? All preferences start with no preferences as we have no idea what we like and don't like. Take for example a baby boy who has never had a scoop of ice cream and is only presented with two choices – a scoop of vanilla ice cream or a scoop of chocolate ice cream. He will most likely choose vanilla one time and chocolate one time (out of curiosity). Preferences then go from a "no preference" state to a "partial preference" state. Back and forth we go until (as we get older) we start picking vanilla (if this is the flavor we realize we prefer) more often than chocolate. Then eventually we go from a "partial preference" to a "full preference" (always picking vanilla) because we simply now know we enjoy that flavor much more than the other. Preferences are built up over time as likes and dislikes become more apparent to oneself (but this also does not prove free will). In this example—we obviously did not choose our taste buds. Another example would be whether you prefer the window or aisle seat when you fly on an airplane. Preferences do not prove free will. Preferences are built up over time and demonstrate/manifest genetic predispositions coming to fruition via actual life (interacting with one's environment). In the example above (as stated), we did not choose our taste buds. Preferences simply highlight how cause and effect rule all of mankind and in fact prove that free will is just an illusion. When we choose something over something else, all we are doing is adhering to the mandatory program we are running in our operating system called "seek pleasure avoid pain" and move towards pleasure and away from pain (also known as pleasure principle). In short, we have no choice but to choose what "we predict" will give us the most amount of greater and greater overall life satisfaction. Now if our "choice" for some reason caused us to suffer, that was certainly not our intention which is why I specifically said, "we predict." The fact that human beings are terrible at predicting things is clearly beside the point. Given the choice, why would you choose to sit in the aisle seat if you knew you much preferred the window seat? And while sitting in the window seat (your full preference), given the choice, why would you order chocolate ice cream if you knew you much preferred vanilla? The answer is you wouldn't and because you do not have free will you actually couldn't. Just because human beings most often do what they want to do does not give them free will. In other words, even though it's true you hardly ever do anything against your will (your wants/ desires), you still do not have free will. This is because we most often can do what we want/desire to do, but we cannot choose _what we_ want/desire to do in the first place. In conclusion: Human Beings are human computers that are programmed to always choose what is predicted to give them more and more overall life satisfaction and this includes avoiding potential harm. Dan Dennett was wrong about this. He said human beings have free will because they are very good avoiders. Are we to believe self-driving cars have free will because they are able to avoid things? Dan Dennett's logic (may he rest in peace) was totally flawed as is true for all so-called *compatibilists. Another definition of Free Will: You/they could have done otherwise. Rest assured, if you/they could have done otherwise, you/ they would have done otherwise. Now a word about so called "choices." Having multiple "choices" or "alternatives" does not grant free will (as they are all not exactly equal in desirability). After we really think about it, and analyze all the possibilities that each choice brings, we soon realize we have a "Hobson's Choice." A Hobson's Choice is a so called "free choice" in which only one choice is really offered because all the other so called "choices" aren't as desirable. So yes, you can make "choices" but not freely so. A) they aren't free from one's personal causal history of how one seeks pleasure and avoids pain (a very personal matter), and B) they are all not exactly equal in desirability. There is always a cause or a reason behind why we select one choice over another, and that reason is not "free will." The cause/reason behind our choice has a cause/reason to that cause/reason and a cause/reason to that cause/reason and a cause/reason to that cause/reason stretching all the way back to before we were conceived/born.

* Some philosophers are called compatibilists because they believe there can still be free will in a deterministic universe. But all they have done is change the definition of free will. Their free will does not involve any actual freedom of choice. They claim such things as a better education give us "more free will." The philosopher Kant called compatibilism "a wretched subterfuge" and "petty word-jugglery."

The Celestine Prophecy being fulfilled by the Insight of No Free Will is not about the illusion of making choices. We know we make choices. This insight is about the illusion of Free Will.

The Celestine Prophecy Fulfilled: The Insight of No Free Will

Insight/Chapter Two

Waking/Competition Hours ("Pragmatic Responsibility") vs Bedtime No Heaven or Hell. Causality and Conditioning.

The Two Levels of the <u>No Free Will</u> Reality:

What time of day is it? <u>It Matters What Time It is:</u>

Before we begin let me define some terms that I will be using for this entire book and what they mean in the context of the new reality of a no-free-will world/society. When I say the words "practical" or "pragmatic" before the word "blame" I am referring to the blameless and faultless type of responsibility and accountability we hold people to on Level One of reality. Level One reality is Waking/Competition Hours aka "pragmatic blame" or pragmatic "blameless or faultless" responsibility/accountability time. These are the hours that we are awake (as opposed to sleeping) that we must battle and compete for human energy (such things as attention and money and other various finite resources) as described in the 1993 book The Celestine Prophecy and subsequent 2006 movie of same name. These "pragmatic blame" Waking/Competition Hours in the no free will world are the hours we must act pragmatically or practically. This is the fake and superficial (tip of iceberg/surface) reality we all must kind of "act as if" and pretend we have free will even though we know we don't have it. It is during these Waking/Competition Hours that we must engage in human energy competition. And because of that we must be able to hold people responsible/accountable for their actions and behavior even in the no free will world (blamelessly so). In short, we must pragmatically blame. Now for Bedtime (all the competing is over with as waking hours has ended). This is just before we go to sleep, and we are no longer interacting or competing with people. This means "pragmatic responsibility" is over with and there is no more competition or battling going on for human energy. This is the fundamental level of reality on which we constantly remind ourselves that free will is an illusion, doesn't exist, and that everything is predetermined. It is Level Two – Bedtime hour (the deepest and truest level) on which all human beings are equally and totally fundamentally innocent like perfect angels and no pragmatic or ultimate responsibility or accountability or blame or fault of any kind is ever assigned to anyone for anything. Once again, (in the no free will world) during the Waking/Competition Hours we assign <u>blameless</u> responsibility (pragmatic "blame") to others (and ourselves) as opposed to the free will world of blameful responsibility to ourselves and others. For example, you don't have to hold a flat tire or malfunctioning robot blamefully responsible to fix it. All you need is "pragmatic" blame (aka blameless responsibility). Human beings will be looked at the same way once everyone knows free will is false.

Then Bedtime (no more competition for anything)…. When we reflect on our day (Bedtime) we now see the fundamental innocence of all mankind. This is the deepest and truest Level of The Ultimate and Final Truth Level of our day. On it we see that we cannot be held responsible (pragmatically or any which way) for our predetermined (determined) behavior of the day. Don't forget, — whether we even reflect on our day (at Bedtime), and how well we reflect on it is also entirely dependent on our personal causal history (nature and nurture) and is predetermined. It's just not spiritually correct to believe in "the buck stops here" assignment of fundamental responsibility for anything that occurs on earth to any human being. While it may be of great pragmatic (Waking/Competition Hours) value to hold people responsible (blamelessly so) for their actions, and to employ systems of reward and punishment, no one is fundamentally deserving of any blame or any praise for anything. One can zoom out and look at the much bigger and broader picture of this mindset which is Waking/Competition Hours is our lifespan here on earth and Bedtime (no more competing for anything) is when we die. Therefore, at Bedtime, we are all equally fundamentally innocent and there is no Judgment Day forthcoming (no Heaven or Hell). This means The Celestine Prophecy is hereby fulfilled as we welcome in the age of No Free Will = No Heaven or Hell. To be clear, this is truly historical and revolutionary. The big evolution of consciousness here and takeaway is that without Free Will there cannot be a Judgment Day on which some of us go to Heaven while others of us go to Hell (God cannot judge a man or woman whose will is unfree obviously). The only way Heaven and Hell could exist is if we are predetermined to go to either one (but this sounds much too unfair, so it also doesn't make much sense). This is a truly history making evolution of consciousness (no Heaven or Hell) that the fulfillment of The Celestine Prophecy is making.

"History is not just the evolution of technology; it is the evolution of thought."

— James Redfield, *The Celestine Prophecy*

One must be careful here and always remember that on the pragmatic Level #1 (Waking/Competition Hours) people must still be held responsible/accountable (blamelessly so) for reconditioning and rehabilitative purposes to keep society safe. Again, you don't have to deeply or truly blame a flat tire or malfunctioning robot to fix it (people like tires or robots obviously don't have free will). All you need is pragmatic blame. In this new no free will world there are two levels of reality both obviously without free will since free will doesn't exist in the first place. Understanding the difference between the pragmatic Waking/Competition Hours blameless/faultless responsibility level and the fundamental level/Bedtime/no more competition Hours of innocence and no responsibility or accountability level is of utmost importance to the Insight of No Free Will. It is job number one in this new no free will world reality, and one must always be hyper aware and cognizant of what level one is discussing this new no free will reality on (Waking/Competition Hours Level or Bedtime Hours Level).

Please note:

Throughout the remainder of this book, I will be using the words <u>Pragmatic</u> to mean Waking/Competition Hours or Level 1 of reality and <u>Fundamental</u> to mean Bedtime Hours or Level 2 of reality.

Causality and Causal chains:

A causal chain is a series of causes leading to an effect. We cannot know all the causes of our choices in any one chain (thanks to the sub/ unconscious), but we can know the cause and effect of a few obvious leading causes. For example: I got drunk and that's why I got into a car accident. But why did you have the desire to drink and drive in the first place? Obvious Causes: Causes we can know. We can readily spot one or a few causes for an event. I parked at a fire hydrant. I got a parking ticket.

Hidden Causes: Causes we can't know. Most of them happened before we were even born, like the impact on your life by the Ottoman Empire, Marco Polo, or Alexander the Great. As stated before, most of the reasons and causes behind our choices are hiding in our sub/unconscious. This is a concept that was popularized by Sigmund Freud. False Causes: Unrelated and improvable causes. This is when we rationalize what we have done in retrospect and just start making stuff up so that it fits neatly into our life paradigm. But we have no proof of it causing anything and invent it after the fact (to make some sense of it all). Most people believe they have free will because they choose things. As we have stated, choosing does not equal free will. Choosing nonetheless is a very real human experience, and we do it a hundred times a day (at least) consciously and mostly unconsciously. Our choices propel us from one place to another, enable us to meet our needs, and give us the feeling that we are creating our lives.

The choosing process usually goes something like this:

Step 1

Options arise. We consider the costs and consequences, pros and cons etc. We always want to pick the option and/or options that will bring us the most pleasure and least pain.

Step 2

We select one or more option(s). As the option(s) becomes stronger and more desirable than the others, we make a choice. Our intuitions and/or hunches often guide us. Intuitions and/or hunches are entirely based on prior intuitions/hunches and whether they ended up being good or bad for us. Intuitions and/or hunches are part of our personal causal history learning curve chain just like everything else is.

Step 3

We act on our choice.

Step 4

We judge the results of our choice. This is how and why we will decide in the future whether to make the same choice or not if the same situation or set of circumstances were to occur.

We live and learn by reflecting on our choices and if we experience a painful outcome, we now know for the next time to choose differently. What if we don't decide? Then we simply made a choice not to make a choice (so it is therefore still a choice). Some people say that their soul or spirit made the choice for them:

How does having a soul or spirit choosing on my behalf give me free will? That doesn't sound like I'm in control of anything. In fact, a non-physical mysterious entity choosing on my behalf would make me feel more out of control than ever.

My Spirit or Soul makes my decisions for me:

A mysterious non-physical entity coming completely out of left field without any reason behind it? On top of that, why doesn't the spirit/soul get conditioned and learn from its mistakes just like every other organ/ system we have? Now, let's say your decision making has led you to experience incredible amounts of pain in your lifetime. Rest assured, if you could have done it differently – you would have. You made the best decision you could with the knowledge and intuition/hunch you had at that moment in time. If you knew a building was going to collapse onto you and kill you before you ran into it to save people, would you still have run in there and sacrificed your life? If yes, why? If not, why not? Yes, you can make a choice, but not freely so. There is always a cause/reason for your choice. While it's true that you can improve upon your performance the next time you're in a similar situation, you can never repeat the past. You can't put your toe in the water the exact same way twice. This is because there are so many moving parts and variables that occur during the passage of time. What you will do the next time is make the best decision you can with the new knowledge you have at that new moment in time (acquired from reflecting on the results of how well you did or didn't do the last time). This is the karmic stream of life. In closing, everything that happens has a cause. Everything you think, say, and do happens because something precedes it. Nothing can appear without being brought about, created, or formed by antecedents or precursors. Furthermore, every effect becomes a cause. Effects don't just lounge around all day without a purpose, cut class, smoke pot, play video games and go into hiding. They do just the opposite. Effects are straight A students with 4.0 GPA's. They very skillfully hover around you like an invisible armada of protective helicopters or hummingbirds making sure your prior mistakes are not repeated. They protect you from making the same exact mistake twice (if they can help it). They provoke other new decisions into action so that history won't repeat itself. Mistakes want you to have learned your lesson(s). The effects of prior causes (your feelings after the past decisions you have made) are extremely powerful creators of new decisions to be made at a time in the future when their relevance is most relied upon. Cause and effect are two sides of the same decision coin that are stored up in our memory banks (consciously and/or sub/ unconsciously) that keep influencing our decision making so on and so forth until the day we die.

Vanilla or chocolate?

We go into an ice cream store and choose Vanilla over Chocolate. It is a seemingly simple choice, and we claim that our taste preference is the cause of this choice. Yet choices are never that simple. *We can choose our preferences, but we cannot choose **what** those preferences are in the first place.*

The choice of Vanilla is influenced not only by taste, but also by color, texture, smell, presentation, and more than likely by earlier pleasant memories of the flavor Vanilla. Compared to other decisions we make in life, deciding which flavor of ice cream to order is a relatively simple one. Other decisions or undertakings such as strategies in war, whether to marry or not, to leave one's job or not, or learning how to play a very complex computer game (or the guitar) are much more complicated. This complexity often involves a multitude of interrelated calculations such as speed and distance ratios, degrees of strength, how much time one has to act, brain to muscle memory, brain chemistry, brain neuroactivity, brain neuroplasticity, and which fingers and/or toes one must use and how hard or not to press them (not to mention how fast they must be moved and at what angle/direction).

Hand eye coordination synapses must be fired off, and neurotransmitters are set off in every conceivable way. All in a micro-second. Neuroscience is forcing us to reconsider all this complexity in a more simplified way. It is simple. Every moment of every action is dependent on the moment before no matter how complex. One moment in time causes the next moment in time. So on and so forth. Pleasure brings about a certain response in the future (more likely to do again) and pain does the same exact thing (more likely to avoid the next time).

Conditioning - Everything Conditions You

Here's a look at the two major conditioning models: Classical and Operant Conditioning.

Classical Conditioning:

The typical procedure for inducing classical conditioning involves presentations of a neutral stimulus along with a stimulus of some significance, the "unconditional stimulus." The neutral stimulus could be any event that does not result in an overt behavioral response from the organism under investigation. Conversely, presentation of the significant stimulus necessarily evokes an innate, often reflexive response. Pavlov called these the unconditional stimulus (US) and unconditional response (UR), respectively. If the neutral stimulus is presented along with the unconditional stimulus, it would become a conditional stimulus (CS). Pavlov used the term conditional because he wanted to emphasize that learning required a dependent or conditional relationship between CS and US. If the CS and US always occur together and never alone, this perfect dependent relationship or pairing causes the two stimuli to become associated, and the organism produces a behavioral response to the CS. Pavlov called this the conditional response (CR). Google Pavlov's Dog to learn more.

Operant conditioning:

While classical conditioning forms an association between two stimuli, Operant conditioning forms an association between a behavior and a consequence. This is what some people refer to as "carrots or sticks conditioning." Carrots are rewards and sticks are punishments. It is also called response-stimulus or RS conditioning because it forms an association between the animal's response [behavior] and the stimulus that follows [consequence].)

Four Possible Consequences

There are four possible consequences to any behavior. They are the following:

Something good can start or be presented; something good can end or be taken away; something bad can start or be presented; something bad can end or be taken away.

The consequences must be immediate or clearly linked to the behavior. With verbal humans, we can explain the connection between the consequences and the behavior even if they are separated in time. For example, you might tell a friend that you'll buy dinner for them since they helped you move, or a parent might explain to a child that she can't go to summer camp because of her bad grades. With very young children (humans who don't have verbal skills) and animals, you can't explain the connection between the consequence and the behavior. For the animal/very young children, the consequence must be immediate.

Technical Terms

The technical term for "an event started" or "an item presented" is positive since it's something that's added to the animal's environment. The technical term for "an event ended" or "an item taken away" is negative since it's something that's subtracted from the animal's environment. Anything that increases a behavior – makes it occur more frequently, makes it stronger, or makes it more likely to occur – is termed a reinforcer. Often, an animal (or person) will perceive "starting something good" or "ending something bad" as something worth pursuing, and they will repeat the behaviors that seem to cause these consequences.

These consequences will increase the behaviors that lead to them; they are reinforcers. These are consequences the animal will work to attain, so they strengthen the behavior. Anything that decreases a behavior – makes it occur less frequently, makes it weaker, or makes it less likely to occur – is termed a punisher. Often, an animal (or person) will perceive "ending something good" or "starting something bad" as something worth avoiding, and they will not repeat the behaviors that seem to cause these consequences. These consequences will decrease the behaviors that lead to them; they are punishers.

Applying these terms to the four possible consequences, you get:

Something good can start or be presented, so behavior increases = Positive Reinforcement (R+)
Something good can end or be taken away, so behavior decreases = Negative Punishment (P-)
Something bad can start or be presented, so behavior decreases = Positive Punishment (P+)
Something bad can end or be taken away, so behavior increases = Negative Reinforcement (R-)

Or

	Reinforcement (behavior increases)	Punishment (behavior decreases)
Positive (something added)	Positive Reinforcement Something added increases behavior.	Positive Punishment Something added decreases behavior.
Negative (something removed)	Negative Reinforcement Something removed increases behavior.	Negative Punishment Something removed decreases behavior.

Remember that these definitions are based on their actual effect on the behavior in question: they must reduce or strengthen the behavior to be considered a consequence and be defined as a punishment or reinforcement. Pleasures meant as rewards but that do not strengthen a behavior are indulgences, not reinforcement; aversives meant as a behavior weakener but which do not weaken a behavior are abuse, not punishment. So, in a nutshell, everything in life is constantly conditioning you one way or another. Described above are the two main conditioning models that happen to us while we are on earth. Don't forget the culture in which you live. The culture conditions you as well. It is not a "direct conditioning model" but rather a more subtle and indirect overall "conditioning model." Conditioning Example: Remember as kids when you and I played baseball or softball for the very first time we ran on contact from first base to second base even though the outfielder had caught the ball. Remember how we learned that made an out. That pain we felt for making a silly out. But if no one had previously properly explained the rule to us, how were we to know? We weren't born knowing that rule. Then we learned we could "tag up" and run to the next base but only after the ball was caught. The prior pain of making an out on this play had conditioned us to learn from our previous base running blunder (mistake). That's how we learn things and get conditioned responses. The next time we were on first base and the ball was hit to the outfield, we then waited on the bag to make sure it wasn't caught before we began running to second base. Then we either "tagged up" or didn't—another learned (conditioned) response. Same external event, different response due to conditioning. Conditioned responses and reflexive or instinctual (innate) responses make us the human beings we are today. Free will is nowhere to be found.

The Celestine Prophecy Fulfilled: The Insight of No Free Will

A More Logical Understanding of Reality

Such things as increasing rates of depression, violence, suicide, wars, revolutions, self-hatred, other hatred, self-blame, other blame, political turmoil, and natural disasters are all symptoms of a planet in a downward spiral. The total cumulative sum effort of all previous generations to build, create, and invest in making our individual journeys through life an overall more peaceful and pleasant experience (while well intended) seem to have failed us miserably. This is because despite all the so-called advances and progressions we have made in such things as technology (thereby increasing the overall material standard of living), it seems we have made very little to no progress at all in the most important aspect of being a human being – the evolution of the human consciousness. The so-called progress we have made in the material world has not been progress at all. It seems that under the "free will" model after every progression (cell phones, email, internet etc.), we have had to go back to try and try again to fulfill ourselves with newer and faster models of everything often resulting in less and less life satisfaction. We find ourselves reverting to the old habits of feeling empty and lost as crucial life lessons remain elusive and unlearned time and time again. In other words, overall life satisfaction is not increasing even though all these technological advances would suggest otherwise. Why is this? What is going wrong? It is the basic belief of The Celestine Prophecy Fulfilled that upon proper reflection of life, the future of the planet, and everyone's contribution (however small it may be), that the foundation of society's collective consciousness is incorrect (the belief in free will). Human beings need a new understanding of reality. This underlying basic foundational consciousness error creates a massive outward ripple effect (aka the butterfly effect) causing more and more untold human misery. It will only continue to get worse and worse unless something new and different comes along and changes the underlying way we collectively perceive and understand the world in which we live in. In short, our collective consciousness simply needs to change because it is currently incorrect (the belief in free will). While it may be difficult to believe at first, it is quite possible that the force of energy emanating from the cataclysmic "big bang," or from any other story of creation may have in fact created a cause and effect chain that predestined the very moment of our birth, every move that we make, every pattern of our existence, every thought that we have, and even the exact moment of our death. This is of course hypothetical speculation just as much as "free will" is hypothetical speculation. Neither is physically provable, but it is indeed time to understand that one version of this story is much more likely and much more <u>logical</u> than the other. The more <u>logical</u> version is that "free will" is an illusion, and just a myth. The "free will" model of reality has had enough time to be tried and tested, and it simply no longer makes any logical sense to believe in such a thing. Not only is the belief in free will illogical, it is also a fairy tale. Believing in free will is as magical a fantasy as believing in Santa Claus. The results of new neuroscience data are now in, and the belief in "free will" simply no longer makes any logical sense. The "unfree will" model is much more logical and easier to prove. The Celestine Prophecy Fulfilled believes that humans now possess the intellectual capacity to understand how and why it is much more likely and logical that a human's will is completely and utterly one hundred percent causal (meaning "unfree"), and that all of life is therefore predetermined. This new insight (of No Free Will) explains the basic premise that man does not possess a "free will," and why this is very good news for society's future. A better world is envisioned as the basic premise that everything has a cause will begin to be implemented into daily life. Quite frankly, it is time to try something different. The free will model of society is simply not working. Look at how much hatred and despair our planet currently has. Let's now create a society based on the logical assumption and correct foundation of reality —that man's will simply not be free. We believe the results of a one hundred percent causal will (no free will) society cannot be any worse than the world we currently live in (so we have nothing to lose). We believe the results of an unfree will society will be far better. We envision a much more understanding and compassionate world. All we ask from you, the reader, is to keep an open mind and give a whole new way of life a chance. This book challenges traditional thinking and forces people to reconsider their notion of "free" will and see their entire self-image in a whole new context. The Celestine Prophecy has been fulfilled with the new huge spiritual breakthrough that Man's Will Is Not Free. Everything that is or is not must be as it is or is not and everything must be as it is, or it would be otherwise. That includes your current belief or disbelief in free will. Everything is happening exactly as it was meant to be throughout the entire universe, from the smallest subatomic particle to the largest and most remote galaxy. Each human life is a small but necessary element of the entire universe. Individual choices are always caused, and it doesn't matter how they are caused. The "I Am" that we are is just a witness to the mind/body as it manifests the will of God (aka the entire universe). We are just passengers along for the ride.

The Celestine Prophecy foretold that we are on the verge of a huge spiritual breakthrough. Th widespread knowledge that man does not possess a free will is the long-awaited fulfillment of The Celestine Prophecy.

On an entirely separate issue, not only does this book fulfill an actual real prophecy (published thirty-two years ago), but it can also be regarded as a unique "self-help" book. This is because most, if not all, other "self-help" books/recovery books/recovery programs all make the same and very faulty assumption – that human beings have free will. These books or recovery programs have simplistic titles like The Seven Spiritual Laws of Succes, 30 Days to a Better You, Secrets of The Millionaire Mind, The Twelve Steps to Sobriety, 100 Days of Weight Loss, The A, B, C method of Cognitive Behavior Therapy (REBT), The Thirty Day Money Workbook, The New Eight Steps to Happiness, or The DBT (dialectical behavior therapy) skills workbook. As stated above, all these recovery programs seem to make the same very faulty and illogical assumption – that human beings have something called "free will" and can just conveniently learn or not learn whatever they want or don't want whenever they want. The authors of these books or recovery programs seem to believe that if we just tried hard enough and followed their certain number of steps or "spiritual laws" (seven, eight, twelve), went to their seminars or forums (the landmark forum comes to mind), read their books for a certain amount of time, mastered their DBT skills manual, or properly learned their A, B, Cs of cognitive behavior therapy (REBT), we are all practically guaranteed a happy and healthy life. Rational Emotive Behavior Therapy (REBT) and all cognitive behavior therapy is based on being "rational." The main DBT (dialectical behavior therapy) goal or concept is to "build a life worth living." If we all had this magical thing called "free will" then why do some of us fail time and time again to attain such things as mental, physical, material, emotional and spiritual health? Nobody would ever fail at The Twelve Steps, Cognitive Behavior Therapy (CBT), REBT, or DBT (dialectical behavior therapy) if we had free will. Everyone who has taken such things as a DBT course would simply learn the skills supposedly needed to feel better. The success rate would be

100%. But not everyone "gets it" no matter how hard they try. Who would ever freely choose to be depressed? How come some people in dialectical behavior therapy (for borderline personality disorder) get well, while others do not? Most, if not all, recovery programs are condensed, written for, and marketed to the "mass market" consumer who just wants some easy steps or skills to follow to attain a certain goal (make more money, lose weight, become less depressed for example). If we all had free will then these "easy steps" or skills we needed to learn, or simplistic A, B, C paradigms to health (REBT) would all be easily attainable as we would all just freely will ourselves to learn them all.

There is nothing more irrational than believing in free will. If everyone could freely choose to build a life worth living because therapists or books told them to do so, they would. With free will, nobody would ever fail at such things as cognitive behavior therapy (CBT), dialectical behavior therapy (DBT), or rational emotive behavior therapy (REBT), yet so many people do. Clearly something is off here. A more logical understanding of reality is needed.

Common sense, logic, and critical thinking/reasoning are always left out of the equation for some reason – until now. This book includes all mankind. It has been written for the regular and average person as well as the intellectual or super intellectual. At this point in the book, to be a free will skeptic (which I sincerely hope you are at this point), all you need is an open mind, logic, and common sense. Hopefully you are lucky enough to have these traits. The Celestine Prophecy Fulfilled has teachings which are very complex but also tries to simplify things wherever and whenever possible. If humans had free will, they would be able to sidestep their brain's programming. People's desires, thoughts, actions, and beliefs would be completely independent of one's genes, memories, environment, and conditioning. All humans would be then left to flounder in a chaotic sea of total and complete indecision. "What shall I do next? I can't make up my mind" would rule each of our moment to moment lives. We would all be little Gods and be first causers. As a powerful first causer we would all become paralyzed with indecision, confusion, emptiness, meaninglessness, and purposelessness. With "free will" our super intelligent genetic code and personal experiences would now be completely erased, and we wouldn't have a clue of what to do next because we would no longer know what we'd prefer doing in any given situation or circumstance. Openly refuting the existence of free will has been a taboo subject for many years now. In fact, I don't think I've ever seen a talk show debating this issue on television or heard one on the radio. Buckle your seat belts people because this is all about to change in a huge way. The free will is an illusion tipping point is coming to a town or city near you real soon. A more logical understanding of reality will sell like hotcakes. Salesmen/women will not be needed because truth and logic easily sell themselves.

The Celestine Prophecy Fulfilled: The Insight of No Free Will

The Word "Free" Confuses

The problem is the word "free." What does the word "free" mean?

Let's look at some common ways the word free is used in the world today. It's very confusing to say the least.

Free riding
Free loading
Buy one get one Free
There is no Free lunch
It's a Free country
I have Freedom of speech
America is the "Land of the Free"
We Drive on the Freeway
I'm a Free man
I'm Free to do whatever I want
Chlorine Free
Sugar Free
Germ Free
Get out of jail Free card
Free as a bird
Free falling
Free Range
Free Throw (Basketball term)
Live Free or die (State of New Hampshire License Plate)
I feel so wild and Free
I'm Free Saturday night for dinner
I own that Free and clear
The quarterback somehow avoided the sack and got Free
Free at last, Free at last, thank God Almighty, I'm Free at last

I'm pain Free
I'm home Free
Free parking
There's no charge. It's Free.
If you love someone, set them Free
Political Freedom
Reproductive Freedom
Social Freedom
Freedom Tower
Let Freedom Ring
I'm independently wealthy and Free to do whatever I so desire
I choose therefore I have free will

And now for the #1 all-time most confusing phrase with the word free in it:

"God gave man free will. But he already knows what you will do because He's all powerful and all knowing."

Now let's discuss why the word freedom is so confusing with regards to the free will issue. Free will being an illusion does not diminish the importance of political, physical, religious, or social freedom. Free will is not required to have a society give its citizens political freedom (freedom of speech, rights to criticize the government, freedom from oppression, freedom to peacefully assemble, right to vote), physical freedom (not being locked up or constrained as to where you can or cannot go), social freedom (freedom of the press, free to marry a person of any race, religion, or gender), or religious freedom (free to practice any religion you want or none at all). All that is needed for human beings to have these things is the ability to seek pleasure and avoid pain otherwise known as greater and greater overall life satisfaction. Free will is not needed. The issue of whether human beings have free will is a completely different matter entirely and should not be confused with other types of freedom.

The USA is the "land of the free" but offers its citizens the same amount of free will as every other country on earth. Exactly zero.

As a society, it would be great to understand and normalize the understanding that such expressions as "of your own free will" and "he's a self-made millionaire or man" are <u>just expressions</u> based on fantasy. These fantasy expressions should really be retired and put out to pasture asap.

We also need to understand how we change when someone pushes us to do so (parents/coaches/teachers/bosses etc.) ... When someone says such things to you like "you could have done better" or that "you could've done that task quicker" what can you say back especially if you did do that task faster and better the 2nd time they asked? Simply say "I did as best I could at the time and as quickly as I could at the time with the data, motivation, desire, and knowledge I had at the time. I did that as quickly as possible and as well as I could at that time.... Now when you started pushing me to do it better and faster my consciousness and motivation then changed (based on the new stimuli/environment I encountered). This new stimuli/environment <u>caused me</u> to do it better and faster (with your coaching), but that was AFTER your domino (new stimuli pushing me) knocked into my domino and created a new cause or reason for me to do so. The new external stimuli (of you pushing me) got me to do that task better and faster." This has nothing to do with free will. It just proves causality.

Speaking of free will and causality, human beings are not "free" to do whatever they want, whenever they want because our actions are causally bound (chain of events). If a dear and respected friend or family member recommended something to you (say a movie), you will most likely go see it. This is called "word of mouth" advertising and is the most effective type of advertising out there. The suggestion or recommendation caused you to do a certain action. This is not "free" will. This is simply a cause creating an action. Now that you've begun to read this book, think about what the cause/reason or causes/reasons were for you to pick up this book in the first place. Now think about what the words "free will" mean to you. Are you reading this book right now because you have free will or because of some reason? What are you seeking by reading this book? You are probably seeking self-realization, truth, and enlightenment. But you are not doing anything at all. You may be the thinker of your thoughts, and the experiencer of your experiences, but you are not self-creating them to occur. They just happen as the cause-and-effect chain (think of a train) keeps deterministically barreling through space and time. "The Choo! Choo! Train of the Causal Chain." You see every moment of the train's movement is directly dependent on the moment of the train's movement the moment before. This is just like your life. Every moment of your life is dependent on the moment before. This is quite easy to understand as every moment of the universe is dependent on the moment before and human beings are part of the universe. "All aboard the Truth Express. Choo! Choo!" There is no credible evidence to support the notion of free will. What would a "free choice/will" decision even look like? It would have to be totally independent of anything that has ever influenced, been taught, or suggested to you. Independent of your biology (genetics) and environment. Independent of your nature and nurture. Yes, you can live quite well knowing that free will is a myth, an illusion. You won't deeply or severely blame people as much nor will you deeply or severely blame yourself as much. You will see reality as it really is — just a bunch of conditioned people walking around making so called "decisions" and manifesting their past experiences (past conditioning and genetics). The Insight of No Free Will as the ultimate fulfillment of The Celestine Prophecy should equal less animosity and acrimony towards ourselves and others. This will happen when we learn to accept that everything was, is, and will be fated. A planet without free will should be a much better planet to live on. Human beings simply do and say what they have been taught to do and say in any given situation or do and say what they feel will give them the most pleasure or least pain in any given situation. People get trained just like animals do except we are a million times more complicated and have a sub/unconscious. Many people make decisions which appear to be uncaused because the cause is unknown to them. This is because the cause is in the sub/unconscious. The Brain is the actual chooser. One could say "My quarks made me do it." Your brain allows you to choose a BMW over a Volkswagen for example. Is that free will? You choose one thing over another due to preferences not because you have free will. Preferences develop over time as a pattern in brain neuro chemistry which is completely dependent on past experiences. Eventually, one pattern passes a certain criteria test for the brain which allows you to choose something over another. It allows you to pick a pizza over a hot dog for example and a trip to Spain over a trip to France. Choosing is an extremely complex, cerebral event. Our brains can store millions of emotional memories, past decisions, and ultimately gives us a "feeling" or an intuition or a "hunch" to do or purchase one item or brand over another. People say, "it just felt or feels right" or "it just felt like the right thing to do at the time." Contrary to public belief – you can't think whatever you want to think about anything. In fact, your entire life is predetermined, and everything was meant to be exactly the way it is now and will be in the future. The experience of choosing is a neural process, with the obvious function of selecting a behavior with its reasonable and foreseeable consequences. It responds to information from the senses, including recommendations, suggestions, advice, and warnings from other people. You cannot step outside your conditioning no matter how hard you may try. From the moment of your conception, your neural grooves began to be honed like an old vinyl record album. Neuro synapses in your brain and throughout your entire body began to form and strengthen. The more you repeated an action, thought or motion, the stronger they became. Some you were born with; some you have acquired throughout your lifetime and some you will continue to acquire as you go through life on the "Truth Express." The personal causal history learning curve chain (train) is the mightiest train of all. "Choo! Choo!" You cannot escape outside the realm of your genetic automatic responses (reflexes) or learned responses by simply "letting them go" or "willing them away." However, one day you may wake up and say, "I need to change my conditioning." How did that happen? Well since every moment of the universe is dependent on the moment before and humans are no exception, then clearly what has happened to your brain state is that "the moment before" was a "moment" in which you realized that you were ready to become aware that your conditioning processes needed to be changed. You had conditioned yourself to believe that you needed re-conditioning. It's still all part of the same causal chain because causal chains can never be broken even if you "choose" to change your conditioning patterns. You might decide for example to only reward yourself if you "do well" at something. You might also decide to punish yourself if you "screw something up." Either way – the time had come for these thoughts, and this has nothing to do with man having a "free will."

Deciding to change one's conditioning is just a moment in time (new thought) dependent on the moment in time before that moment in time (thought before new thought). It has nothing to do with having free will. What a train of thought this insight was. Choo! Choo!

Deciding does not mean we have "free will" even if that decision is to change one's conditioning. All decisions/actions are dependent on the moment before. This is as true for human beings as it is for the train on a train track or the entire state of the universe.

The Celestine Prophecy Fulfilled: The Insight of No Free Will

Benefits and Insights

What are some of the benefits of understanding that free will is a myth? For starters excessive and overly severe punishment and revenge seeking will go away because humans are not deeply, truly, or fundamentally to blame for anything. Overly harsh scapegoating in things like sports radio talk shows and call-in-shows will also go away so people like the Bill Buckners and Steve Bartmans of the future world won't have to worry about death threats and go into hiding. Not to mention getting killed/murdered like Andres Escobar was after his own goal in the 1994 World Cup. Just turn on your local sports radio talk show and listen to all the current out of control overly harsh scapegoating that goes on each night. Overly harsh and severe blaming, shaming, and scapegoating is a secret menace that hurts and ruins our society. Another benefit of the No Free Will Insight is the flip side of all that hate mentioned above… that being false worship, idolizing, pride, arrogance, and conceit will also go away because we humans are not fundamentally praiseworthy since nothing is up to us (it's all luck). This eliminates people being able to feel superior and hence looking down on others. Look what I did, I'm a hero! I deserve special treatment now because after all I deserve it after what I did! I deserve a medal! I deserve a super large raise! Understanding free will is false, eliminates over idolizing and putting people on an overly exaggerated unrealistic hero pedestal in which they are to be worshipped like a little God. Making people into Godlike heroes is just as unrealistic as demonizing them. In summary, the no free will insight eliminates toxic and abusive excessive blame (towards yourself and others) and toxic and unrealistic excessive praise (towards yourself and others) as no one is in fundamental control of their own lives. When you deeply blame and resent someone or something (or yourself), what you are really saying is "they/I should have been able to rise above their/my circumstances and conditioning and done the 'right thing' by me. All they/I had to do was simply make use of their/my 'free will' and behave like a 'good' person. Since they/I didn't choose to act that way, they/I am a 'bad' person. I/they deserve to suffer and be punished!" We all know that when a baby is born it could not have a free will and needs to be taught everything about life. So, when exactly would "free will" start? At what age? 6? 12? 16? 19? And if it did start suddenly out of nowhere – how would you know? How could you tell? What would the signs be? What would "free will" suddenly look like? We humans are not acknowledging a fundamental truth about our existence when we believe in free will. As a species we owe it to ourselves to get this right once and for all. This will create a planet of more compassion and understanding towards our fellow man as we all begin to evolve consciously to a place where we can all talk about what we are experiencing here more accurately.

Some Insights:

In the future, the humans of a not-too-distant tomorrow, will consider us in the "dark ages" of consciousness and will find it almost comical that it took us this long to finally realize free will does not and cannot exist. On the other hand, they won't be able to judge us because we had no choice in the matter as to how, why, or when the free will illusion bubble will finally burst. Free will's illusory bubble will pop and burst when it's meant to be (just like everything else in life). It's in the hands of fate as I write this. As you go through life, you will constantly be conditioned by experiences and information. You will make choices that are not free, but are based on prior information, conditioning, and determinants. Free will implies that there are choices in life that are exactly 50/50. To be clear that means 50.000000 to infinity versus 50.000000 also to infinity. That's simply impossible. Nothing is ever exactly 50/50. By this I mean two choices are never exactly equal. One choice will inevitably seem "better" to us after a good long while of thinking about it. This is not because we have free will. This is simply because we have a conditioned preference built up inside us over time.

Once we go through the process of living and thinking, we will always inevitably find one choice is better for us than the others.

A 50/50 choice would make us in essence a "first causer" which would make us a little God. In other words, all decisions were and are inevitable once we go through the process of living. Just because we do not possess free will does not mean we cannot enjoy the already made movie that is our life. This is because there are so many twists and turns and so many unexpected things that happen to us that we soon realize the joy of living is how the story unfolds (how the story is told is why we go to the movies).

The best story tellers are the best movies and vice versa.

There are only two types of people in the world. Those who believe in free will and those who do not. If you believe you have an infinitesimally small amount of free will even .000000000000001% then you are in fact a free will believer. Not believing in free will (like I do) means all human beings have exactly zero free will.

Attraction isn't a choice. As humans, we don't "consciously choose" who we feel attracted to. It just "happens" to us... Bang! And you can't convince someone to feel this powerful emotion. Quite often (most of us can relate to this), attraction doesn't make any logical sense to us on the surface level (so much of our conditioning is stored in our unconscious/subconscious). When you think about the concept of being attracted to another person (physically or emotionally), it only makes sense that you should feel attracted to good qualities like kindness, honesty, and loyalty, right? Then why do we fall for people who lack everything we say we are looking for? A human's lack of free will is most apparent in the dating world. Nobody would "freely choose" to suddenly fall out of love with someone. Nobody would "freely choose" to get a divorce if it were up to them. Attraction clearly isn't freely willed. There is no logical sense of who we are attracted to and who we are not attracted to. Call it timing. Call it chemical. Call it biological. Call it fate. Whatever you call it, it certainly cannot be called "free" will.

One more Insight:

Question: How could someone prove free will?

Answer: They can't because it doesn't exist but…. in theory… the only real way to prove free will existed would be to rewind the entire state of the universe and see what happens. If there were free will, events would turn out differently once we pressed play again. After all, people could "freely choose" to act otherwise. It is because free will is false that everything would turn out the exact same way it did the first time.

The Celestine Prophecy Fulfilled: The Insight of No Free Will

The Law of Causation Creates Fundamental Vindication

It is generally believed that our sense of free will presents an interesting dilemma: on the one hand, it is difficult to make sense of it in purely causal terms; on the other hand, we *feel as if we are the* creators of our own actions. It's like asking what came first, the chicken or the egg? I think that this confusion is a symptom of our dilemma. We are going about this all wrong. If free will is in fact a grand illusion, then our entire investigative process into this matter is distorted to begin with. It's like trying to figure out a magic trick in a hallway full of smoke and mirrors. Why is that? That is because we tend to ask so-called religious/philosopher/scientist experts for their opinion on this free will matter when they themselves are free-will believers and advocates (except for the very few like Sam Harris and Robert Sapolsky). They must sell books/seminars after all. Not only that, but they lack an unbiased and unprejudiced opinion on this matter because they themselves exhibit wishful thinking and motivated reasoning. As stated at the very beginning of this book, this quote from Upton Sinclair always seems to ring true. ***"It is difficult to get a man to understand something when his salary depends on his not understanding it."*** So, the very people we entrust with telling us the ultimate truth have the most to lose by telling us the ultimate truth. This inherent conflict of interest totally and completely taints and distorts their ability to see and speak the truth that free will is false. These "experts" fear (and rightly so) that people will then question their high salaries and high standing in society since life is all luck and therefore any income inequality/disparity can be looked at as undeserving and immoral. In short, they simply cannot say free will is false. It's high time that a regular person (me) with nothing to lose or gain (except hopefully a lot of book sales) stands up to all these liars and so-called "experts." The poor and lazy need and are worth defending. Our experience is not merely delivering a distorted view of reality, but it is also creating the faulty way in which we go about trying to discover the truth. This is why for many years I have read many authors, religious and spiritual leaders, and philosophers debate the issue. I have found time and time again; they all practice the art of "confusionism" (as in a total state of confusion) or circular reasoning. Let's look at par exemplar of this:

Religious/Spiritual leader says:

"God gave you free will. But he already knows what you will do." – What a bunch of nonsense and BS this whole free will thing is. How can you have free will if God knows what you are going to do? Example: I'm at a fork in the road. I can go left or right. God knows I will go left. I decide to go right.… oops I can't go right because God already knows I will go left so I must change my mind at the last second and now must decide to go left because I was never free to freely choose to go right in the first place. This means all they do is confuse people when the answer is so very simple. As just stated, they love to tell people "You have free will" yet "God is in control of everything." Well, which is it? Pick a side for once. Stop the free will flip flopping and double talk insanity. Let's be crystal clear. You do not have free will. Period. Clear enough? All we must do to unravel this do I or don't I have a free will question is simply pay very close attention to what it is like to be ourselves in the world. For example, look at the manifesto written by mass murderer Elliot Rodger and/or pay very close attention to the movie Joker (the first one from 2019). It's all cause and effect and both show how neither Elliot Rodger nor Arthur Fleck had control over their causes (how hurt and alone they felt) or their effects (the subsequent anger and rage they felt). What came first? The chicken or the egg type of debating gets everybody confused and all of us back to square one with nothing accomplished.

Did I cause that? or did that cause me? will now mercifully end. For example, in Elliot Rodger's very detailed manifesto he says "All I ever wanted was to fit in and live a happy life amongst humanity, but I was cast out and rejected, forced to endure an existence of loneliness and insignificance all be**cause** . . . I didn't want things to turn out this way, but humanity **forced my hand**, and this story will explain why . . . I didn't ask for this. I didn't want this." Since Elliot Rodger knew he was "twisted" and even titled his manifesto "My Twisted World" why didn't he stop himself? Answer: No Free Will. Also, on page 109 Elliot says, "I couldn't believe my life was actually turning out this way." He expresses surprise to find himself at a gun shooting range planning a massacre. He couldn't believe that he was beginning to plan for his "day of retribution." Why was he surprised to be there you ask if he was the one wanting to be there? How could he be surprising himself you ask? After all nobody was forcing him to be there right? Right and wrong. No one person was forcing him to be there, **but he was compelled by the entirety of the universe to be there**. He was just a witness to his own life and he knew it (hence his surprise that things were "actually turning out this way"). Being just a witness to our own life is true for all of us. We are all compelled by the big bang (or any other story of creation) to do what we must do. We are all just along for the ride playing out our assigned roles. Conclusion: No Free Will. The moment we do pay attention, very close attention, we begin to see that free will is **just a feeling, just a sensation.** No more, no less. The illusion of free will is just that, an illusion. All one needs to do to get to the bottom of this seemingly complex issue is to understand the very simple law of causation. The "causal chain" rules all of mankind. Everything has a cause/reason. Whether or not you are conscious of the cause/reason or causes/reasons is an entirely separate issue discussed in much more detail in Insight/Chapter Ten.

Spoiler alert, it is totally irrelevant whether or not you are aware of the cause/reason. All you need to know is that there is a cause or reason as to why you do what you do, and that human action is never uncaused or without some sort of reason or rationale. The cause/reason is very likely unknown to you as it is hiding in the sub/unconscious. People who believe in free will incorrectly believe that voluntary behavior (as opposed to mandated behavior) can occur...but how? They insist that free will means that man must be the "ultimate" or "originating" cause/originator of his actions. According to these nonsensical free will believers, humans must have the Godlike power and the magical ability to be ***<u>causa sui</u>** (the cause of itself, self-caused). To be truly and deeply to blame or praise (ultimately and fundamentally) for one's choices one must be the first cause of those choices, where the first cause means that there is no antecedent cause of that very first cause. The argument, then, is that if man has free will, then man is the ultimate cause of his actions -- this means man is the "first causer" and has free will via first mover "agent causation." Therefore, it follows, we all must be little Gods. What nonsense! Are you a little God? I think not.... So, are we back to what came first, the chicken or the egg? No. No, we are not. Once again and in simple terms – the law of causation reigns supreme. There is always <u>A WHY</u> as to why we make the "choices/decisions" we do. The WHY (cause/reason) is always the same and that is to make the best choice we can for ourselves at the time (with the data we have at the time). Therefore, there is no need to argue with philosophy professors, religious/spiritual leaders, or academic types any longer. As stated above, all they will do is confuse you and practice the art of "confusionism" on you. Circular reasoning (not the truth) appears to be their real specialty. Not only that, but when you argue with these PhDs and other high ranking pro-free will belief academic/religious types they unwittingly prove there is no free will by using big fancy words. These big fancy words and very specific religious terminology/jargon are mumbo-jumbo/gibberish/woo-woo science and logic to the regular person and that is exactly because we do not know these words/terms/concepts they are spewing as they are not a part of our working vocabulary and current personal learning curve causal history (we have not studied them and hence do not have advanced degrees in this subject matter). Why is that? You guessed it…. Because there is no free will. These big fancy words were not in our nature and nurture and that's why we haven't a clue as to what these "geniuses" are saying. Ironically, they are trying so hard to salvage and rescue free will with this law of attraction example to manifest this or that, this quantum physics example, and that ontological example, and this epistemological example, and that "infinite potential/quantum cosmic consciousness" concept that they end up unintentionally and unwittingly hitting a home run for the other team. Our team, the no free will team. They highlight our exact point of no free will by trying so hard to prove and demonstrate what geniuses they are. In reality, no one has a clue what they are saying. Ever listen to Deepak Chopra? His "woo-woo" science is so convincing because no one knows what the hell he is even saying. He (and others like him) intimidate you and make you feel free will must be real because after all these guys know much bigger and fancier words than you do. Knowing fancy words and having well-rehearsed answers to why there is or isn't free will just proves and shows that how well we can explain, present, and articulate things is also still part of our personal causal history learning curve (no free will). What can you say back to all these so-called experts? Just say "If I had a free will, I'd understand what you are saying." The point is the topic of proving or not proving free will is no exception to this rule that everything must have a cause or reason behind it. It's quite surreal to think that the actual words used in the free will vs no free will debate are predetermined to begin with. It's self-revealing as words are used in the free will debate itself that some people were taught growing up while others were not. In short, how you argue for it or against it is also still predetermined. What if I told you that the "Law of Ascacomongen" proves this point very well. The "Law of Ascacomongen" has been proven time and time again and there is no doubt that it is true. Would you know what I meant? Of course not, I just made it up. See no free will. But what if the "Law of Ascacomongen" was a real law of reality that you had just never heard before because it wasn't <u>yet</u> in your personal causal learning curve otherwise known as prior nature and/or nurture? Then this just proves that how well I can explain something to you and how well you can understand what I am trying to explain to you is also predetermined because it is entirely dependent on your personal causal past. If predeterminism or simply put determinism is true, then all of man's choices are caused by events and feelings that were there before he made his choice not after. The law of causation is that simple. The only question is what was the first cause? That nobody will ever know. What we do know however is that man was not the first cause because humans were not part of the universe before it was created (or if it's been here forever and ever). The universe is way older than mankind. We were either created through such things as the story of creation or evolution. We simply weren't here first to cause anything in any scenario. So, if everything man does is caused by events, facts, and feelings outside his control, then he cannot be (by definition) the ultimate self - causer of his thoughts, feelings, beliefs, and actions. All the relevant features of a person's inner life such as emotions cause behaviors. Again, it's quite a simple equation. Beliefs = thoughts = emotions = behaviors. So where do the beliefs come from? Once again – the law of causation is the answer. Causality is the relationship between an event (the *cause*) and a second event (the *effect*), where the second event is understood to exist because of the first. <u>We are not born with beliefs or a belief system.</u> Beliefs are taught to us once we are born by such methods as modeling others (for example our parents), verbally taught to us, or a myriad of other ways we form our "paradigm" or belief system about the world. So even though I may not be able to know exactly where or why my beliefs or thoughts come to me as they do (don't forget about the sub/unconscious), I can rest in the peace and knowledge that something has caused them to be the way they are due to the law of causation. The sub/unconscious is also always at play here, so that is yet another reason why we cannot pinpoint with accuracy where or why our beliefs and thoughts are the way they are. Just because you don't know exactly what the cause or causes are for your behavior(s), doesn't mean they don't exist. They do. It's just that you don't know what they are, that's all. Many people seem to feel that quantum mechanics has liberated the human mind from the prison of determinism. They say there is proof in quantum mechanics of uncaused effects. I say that is impossible. There are only two answers to this quantum mechanics/physics argument. One – there are hidden variables or laws not yet discovered causing the outcomes to be what they are (remember the last quark was only discovered a few decades ago and the Higgs Boson was also recently discovered). In the grand scheme of things, these discoveries are quite recent. Isn't it extremely arrogant to think that we've discovered all the subatomic particles that could ever be and that there will be no new discoveries forthcoming? For example, Google newly discovered exotic particles such as the pentaquark and tetraquark. Or Two – everything is random. If everything is random that still doesn't mean we have free will. So as far as the Quantum Mechanics argument goes, The Celestine Prophecy Fulfilled has two answers and here they are (once again as per above):

#1 *hidden variables/hidden laws not yet discovered proving determinism true or #2 everything is random. Either way there's No Free Will. *Gerard't Hooft (Nobel Prize in Physics 1999) also firmly believes that there should be a deterministic theory underlying quantum mechanics. For the record, this entire Quantum Mechanics argument is not even relevant to our discussion because Quantum Mechanics makes no difference. Some people argue that cause and effect doesn't apply to sub-atomic particles. Assuming the indeterminism of these particles could somehow affect human behavior, this would serve only to make human behavior random. Random behavior is clearly not free will.

Now back to causality. Let's look at a real-world example: You go over to your friend's house and he accidentally falls down a flight of stairs and loses consciousness. He's barely breathing. You then begin to frantically call 911 for help. You rush to his side feeling an intense desire to help. Your "self" now seems to stand at the intersection of what to do and what not to do. Should you try CPR? Do you take his pulse to see if it's normal? Should you put him in your car and rush him to the hospital or wait for the ambulance? Should you call your next-door neighbor who you know is a doctor? From this point of view, one can easily see how **one can feel as if** he is the lone source of his own thoughts and actions. You need to quickly decide on what to do and what not to do. **You seem to be an agent acting** of your own free will. The problem is that this point of view cannot be reconciled with what we know about the human brain. We now know that every moment your brain is dependent on the moment before. This basically means you are trained in certain things and not trained in others. Do you even know how to do CPR? Do you even know how to take someone's pulse? Do you even know what a normal pulse rate would feel and sound like? You see, what are your causes? What have you been taught in the past? What have you been told? Practiced? Trained in? What or which neuro-pathway grooves in your brain have been created? All these prior causes will determine what you do in such a crisis as stated above. This is your skill set under pressure basically. You have skill sets that you have learned and built up over time. Some skill sets you can access under pressure and others you cannot. Some skill sets help people survive under the harshest of circumstances while others perish (for example see movie 127 Hours from 2010). The ones who perish simply didn't have the skill set to survive that circumstance. To be clear and to simplify, our behavior can be traced to biological events happening in the synapses of our brains. The law of causation is the first and only law needed to understand why free will is an illusion. Randomness: If I were to learn that my decision to take the bus this morning was due to a random release of neurotransmitters in my brain (as opposed to walking which I do 99.9% of the time), how could the indeterminacy of the initiating event count as me exercising my free will? Such indeterminacy, if it were generally effective throughout my brain, would destroy any semblance of human responsibility. Say while on that bus, another random release of neurotransmitters in my brain were set off and I attacked the bus driver while we were in motion. This indeterminacy of totally random behavior of me now attacking the bus driver will most likely cause a terrible accident. Say this terrible accident killed twenty-five people (but not myself). Obviously, the loved ones of the deceased would "blame" me because I'm the one who attacked the bus driver and caused the accident in the first place. It is safe to say I will be going to jail for a very long time or might even face the death penalty for such a heinous crime. But if I could prove that my behavior was due to a random release of neurotransmitters in my brain – how could I be held responsible? It wasn't my fault that I have this "random release of neurotransmitters in my brain" condition. My attorney would argue the point that my will wasn't free since it was due to a "random release of neurotransmitters in my brain" and there was nothing I could do to stop it from happening. For pragmatic and reasons of utility (usefulness), I would be separated from society because I would be a danger to "myself or others." But fundamentally (in the eyes of The Lord God and hopefully the progressive newspapers of tomorrow), I am still fundamentally innocent. The progressive papers of tomorrow will say: "You can still fear someone, but you just can't hate them. This person is blamelessly responsible." Now imagine what your life would be like if all your actions, intentions, desires and beliefs were all "self-generated" or "first caused" in the fairy tale, imaginary, illusory, and magical so-called "free will" way — well then you would scarcely seem to have a mind at all.

Your life would be totally and utterly rudderless. You would be beyond lost and unable to make any decision(s) at all since they would all seem equally good to you. You wouldn't learn from your mistakes and your decision making would be complete madness. With "free will" all choices would look exactly equal. You would no longer have any preferences. How would you know what to do next? The answer is you wouldn't. "Free Will" causes complete madness. <u>It is only because we don't have free will that anything gets done at all</u> (just the opposite of what most people think). Actions, intentions, beliefs, and desires can only exist in a system that is significantly constrained by patterns of behavior and the laws of stimulus-response (law of causation). How is it that we can communicate with other human beings? How is it that you can read what I am writing? To find my teachings and writings comprehensible at all one needs to recognize patterns and draw on past experiences of what something means. What if I wrote jf kw f=wfsf k;slkkdjf hen knd nn—d=o=e\e\\c — (just like my prior example of The Law of Ascacomongen). Would you know what that meant? To communicate at all means the law of causation: It all depends on the assumption that my thoughts when written will obediently conform to a shared reality (that being more or less correct English grammar we all learned in school). So in this perspective, Heisenberg's "self-generated" mental events would amount to utter ramblings of an incoherent author who next sentence would look something like this: eohjrewjf hsdjh; js;kldnw, =-\\w\w) (* *(8-9&*()&*04i oko;k;lsgkndgi0-8- I80*(0-i9=9 kflsk psd=\=\\p\\p-\?;klk" To see that the addition of randomness – quantum mechanical or otherwise – does nothing to change the situation that our wills are not free and our lives are not up to us. The law of causation makes it possible for you to read this sentence and understand what the "law of causation" even means. There is a cause to you understanding how to read English and a cause for me on how to write a teaching in English. If the law of randomness not causation ruled the universe the next sentence would be ksakjf ksjf;' j[-23]=2r=2- r\204iir 40-ri 2i0r. Do subatomic particles have free will? I think not. Neither Quantum Mechanics nor such things as The Heisenberg Uncertainty Principle salvage free will and to imply otherwise is simply incorrect. Now for how the law of causation creates fundamental vindication and how and why having a causal will creates a better world. If people can come to the truth about their lack of control over how others feel about them, how others treat them, and most importantly how we feel about ourselves, then people's severe guilt, severe blame, severe resentment, and overall severe acrimony (and all other severe and intense negative emotions) will instantly become modified. Severe toxic guilt, blame, acrimony and resentment all go hand and hand with the belief that human beings have free will. We all need to be able to feel healthy modified or moderated guilt (no free will Level 1 Waking/Competition Hours blameless guilt) otherwise known as "pragmatic or practical guilt."

This pragmatic guilt, blame, or resentment comes from the feeling of actual wrongdoing (internal moral code). This way we can correct our behavior (and the behavior of others) for the future. But "severe free will" toxic guilt is not good for anyone. Not good for you, not good for me, and most importantly not good for society. You see, you can move beyond "severe free will" toxic emotions by understanding that free will is an illusion and modify all emotions to a more modified and simply useful and pragmatic level. The "free will" belief that you can freely choose or control your feelings and behavior by doing things "right" –> leads to . . . leads to an overly harsh and severe self-judgment about how well you can control your own behavior and feelings to get yourself to do it "right" –> leads to . . . which leads to severe emotional and toxic guilt (severe self-blame, severe self-resentment or severe self-loathing) when you inevitably do something wrong. The way out of these severe emotional and toxic feelings is to simply understand that free will is an illusion and doesn't exist on any level of reality. With practice, you can eliminate your severe and toxic guilt (and all other severe negative emotions). Practice makes progress and it takes practice, conditioning, and training to constantly remind oneself of the very harmful consequences of believing that humans have "free will." The more you practice your belief that there is no free will, the more progress you will make in freeing yourself from such severe and toxic emotions such as hate and envy. After years of research on subjects ranging from toddlers to sailors to Tibetan monks, neuroscientists are now increasingly concluding that causal brain activity underlie all human emotionality. The formation of our decision making is a causal process. Hence our preferences and our decisions are caused. Others may believe it was possible for us to make other decisions. They tell us "you could have done" this or that or "you should have done" this or that. Or if you "would have only" done this or that. Other people are not you. They are mere outsiders and not privy to what your unique causal antecedents make you, you. They are completely ignorant of your entire decision-making process. If they were you and had the same exact atoms, brain, spirit, soul, and consciousness then they would have done what you did (because they would <u>BE YOU</u>).

But they are not. For other people to claim that we could have decided and done otherwise is completely incoherent. They are making the big mistake of putting their mind into our life! These people seek to impose their internal private life paradigms or world view upon yours. It is completely unwarranted for one human being to tell another human being what they could have done differently or how they could have behaved otherwise. It's ok to gently admonish someone to modify and change their behavior for the next time, but it is not ok to tell someone how they could have done otherwise and differently in the past. Other people do not share your options (or lack of options). They do not share your modus operandi, your genetics, or your past experiences. In short, they have no idea what it's like to be you. Only you do. What we choose to do is never out of "free choice" but was always out of necessity.

Everything that happens is followed by something else which depends on it by causal necessity. Likewise, everything that occurs is preceded by something with which it is causally connected. Nothing can exist or has come into existence in the entire universe without a cause. In short, you can choose your desires, but you cannot choose what your desires are in the first place. We are simply lucky to have moral desires that we act on and are simply unlucky to have immoral desires which we act on. It is because we are not in control of what our desires are in the first place that we are hereby fundamentally (on the truest and deepest level) vindicated. All your past mistakes are hereby vindicated.

Because of the illusion of free will (the law of causation), Heaven and Hell either don't exist or people are predetermined to go to either one. God cannot judge a man or woman without free will. No Free Will = No Judgment Day = No Heaven or Hell. This is most likely the most monumental revelation realized by the evolution of human spiritual consciousness that The Celestine Prophecy so boldly foretold would occur.

The Celestine Prophecy Fulfilled: The Insight of No Free Will

The Myth of Free Will

Each of us lives in a difficult to predict present and near future, which includes our own behavior in it, and which therefore makes our behavior feel spontaneous and undetermined/uncaused—but what we don't experience, yet which are just as real, are the multitude of un/ subconscious influences and determinants of what we think, act, and feel (from our past). Many people argue with me and say, "I have free will because it feels like I have it." I tell them – "just because you feel or believe you have or are something does that make it true? If you feel or believe you're right about something, are you always proven correct? Haven't you ever felt something to be true, yet it wasn't?" Just ask anyone who has ever been in a romantic relationship and "felt" it was "true love" but it didn't work out. Feelings are not facts. Plain and simple. We often believe that if we wish hard enough for something it will come true. We twist and distort the facts to fit what feels best to us on the inside. We rationalize everything to make ourselves feel better. If it feels better internally to believe in the nonsensical belief of free will then that is what we will end up believing in. On the other hand, if it feels best for us internally to believe that free will is a myth and an illusion then that is what we will end up believing. Somehow— I believe the truth will inevitably make us feel better (once we understand it).

Most, if not all people, prefer truth to illusion. They just need the truth properly explained to them. Copernicus, Galileo, and Columbus are all examples of how the truth wins out once the facts are made crystal clear. I don't see why free will being an illusion will be any different.

So why does the truth matter? Because our survival in this high-tech world depends on our being honest with ourselves, on understanding who we really are, as our true nature. In primitive societies, illusions and pseudoscience had benefits. Today is different and people know it. They can feel it, and they can sense it. As The Celestine Prophecy foretold, the evolution of consciousness is the next step for mankind as we become more and more aware of the truth of how human lives are actually lived in reality. It's as if we are at the same magic show getting tricked repeatedly by the same exact illusion. At some point, the collective consciousness (aka "The People") are going to say "enough with that trick already—we are sick of it! We've seen it a million times already and it just doesn't trick us anymore!" Let's move on now because we are now ready for some truth. Illusions at a magic show can be fun for a while, but sooner or later, the smoke and mirrors stuff become tiresome. The Illusion of Free Will is now tiresome. It's worn out. The time has come to put it to rest. The understanding that free will is an illusion and total nonsense gets rid of a lot of negative consequences. Instead of extreme and severe blame, regret, rage, resentment, revenge, envy, and an escalating culture of an "eye for an eye" mentality which is a never ending sequence of violence and hatred (for example as described in Elliot Rodger's My Twisted World manifesto), people will instead blame the universe or the entire cosmos for their misfortune (not themselves or other people) or even better just accept "it is what it is, it's my fate." You can still be pragmatically upset at someone of course, but you will also know concurrently that fundamentally they simply couldn't help themselves (even if they have hurt you terribly). People will understand the difference between severe and extreme emotional blame (free will mindset) and practical, logistical, or pragmatic "blame" (no free will mindset aka blameless responsibility). People (once they understand free will is false) will have no choice but to understand the idea of "blameless or faultless responsibility." People now knowing that free will is one big lie, will still feel pragmatic guilt (we need that to correct mistakes we've made), but future humanity will be spared life threatening and life piercing deep personal shame or embarrassment (caused by the belief that we and others have free will and could have done otherwise). Severe emotional blame (with free will) makes you hate someone so much you want to kill them. Practical or pragmatic "blame" (blameless responsibility with no free will) allows you to "pragmatically blame" them and sue them (to get what you feel is fair in the situation at hand), but without the severe internal emotional turmoil that eats you up inside when you attribute free will blame onto yourself or onto someone else.

Review of The Two Levels of the No Free Will World:

As we learned in Insight/Chapter Two - You will always remember the difference between the 2 Levels of No Free Will – #1 The fake/superficial/surface pragmatic level of reality (holding people blamelessly/faultlessly responsible/accountable) — aka Waking/ Competition Hours Level 1 of Reality and the #2 Fundamental Level (deep/true) nature of people aka Bedtime Level 2 of Reality (no more competition, no ultimate responsibility moral or otherwise and fundamental innocence for all). People who believe in "free will" are blind to the truth and cannot see either level or layer of the no free will world reality (Level 1 pragmatic level or Level 2 fundamental level). This is because free will believers only see what they so desperately want to see – the fairy tale/make believe magical fantasy world of we all have free will. These people (the vast majority) are totally and completely fooled, tricked, convinced by and lost in the illusion that is free will. These people (free will believers) surely practice "blameful responsibility" and want to see the other person severely punished. They want revenge and retribution. They want to see others severely punished to the point of severe suffering (lifetime in jail/death penalty/torture/banish their souls to hell for all eternity).

This causes an escalating cycle of hatred in mankind (think Elliot Rodger). People who know "free will" is an illusion (me for example) will practice Waking/Competition Hours Level 1 "blameless or faultless responsibility" otherwise known as pragmatic "blame." They want admonishment, deterrence, rehabilitation, restraint and/or removal (for safety reasons and rightly so). They want to see others "learn their lesson" (removed from society/sent to jail) to make sure it will never happen again but that's where it ends (not to mention jails should be made a little nicer – but that's a story for another time). They (me) want to see others reconditioned, rehabilitated, and then reconsidered (and be able) to rejoin society. Kind of like a pit stop in an auto race (could be a very long pit stop though like forty years). If you are deemed unfixable, then society will in fact retire you (permanently remove you from the race as your car is too dangerous to drive with the others) and permanently remove you from society as society must be kept safe. Would you allow a <u>permanently</u> defective car or malfunctioning robot (a person) on the road/street with defective wheels/legs (driving/walking around very dangerously) that just can't be fixed? Non-free will believers want punishment only for deterrent purposes and not for revenge or retribution. Free-will believers, in contrast, seek revenge and retribution and way overly severe punishments (like torture and banishing people to hell for all eternity) to make people suffer more and more even well after they have already learned their lesson and have already been deterred more than enough. Which way do you think will create a better society? Why did you choose what you did? What was the cause of your decision? Everything must always have a cause or reason.

You technically can't blame the universe either for it is also causally chained, but it's sure a lot better than blaming fallible people. The universe is a cause-and-effect robotic monster of epic proportions.

How can the discovery that "free will" is total, complete, utter insanity and nonsense help us? What are the benefits and how can it make us all feel better? When someone behaves badly, or even violently, or more to the point heinously lying like a Bernie Madoff situation, the son (Mark) would probably still feel pragmatic shame, but not to the point (severe emotional and fundamental shame) that he would end up committing suicide.

He would've been able to simply tell himself "my father simply couldn't have acted any other way. He had conditioned himself to get away with it and there was no turning back to his unchecked greed. He did not have free will. It was all fated to be that way." If Mark Madoff did not attribute free will to his father (or himself for that matter) I'm sure he'd be alive today.

The same would be true for that Chicago Cubs fan in 2003 who instinctively interfered with a catchable ball that cost his team a crucial out. In the future, when people are raised, taught, and learn that they don't have free will, a more compassionate society will then foster and grow. Therefore, when a situation arises like The Cubs fan, instead of the severe and unnecessary emotional reaction (free will based mindset) of pelting him with beer and obscenities and making the poor fellow go into hiding (at least he didn't die like Mark Madoff although he did get death threats), people will always know deep down that it was just (unfree will based mindset) fate causing him to ***play the role as the scapegoat.*** Each fan would be more compassionate because they would also know deep down that it could have just as easily been them sitting in that chair reaching for that ball. The entire way we view reality will change once we understand that free will doesn't exist. Understanding the difference between severe emotional blameful seething blame (free will based society) and pragmatic blameless responsibility "pragmatic blame" (unfree will based society) will signify the beginning of the long-awaited evolution of human consciousness that The Celestine Prophecy foretold would occur. Understanding something called [1*] "the universe compelled pragmatic pursuits of perceived fair exchanges of human energy" will then be the next domino to fall in the great crumbling of the "delusional free will age" that we currently live in. The same would be true for so called "villains" and "heroes." Instead of a society that over demonizes their "villains" and over decorates and idolizes their "heroes," we would become a society that would understand that the individual in question was simply exhibiting his/her past experiences and genetics (nature and nurture). I'm not saying there aren't "good" guys and "bad" guys. All I am saying is that these people we call good or evil were just fated to be so. They did not freely will it upon themselves (to be good or evil) and that really needs to be understood better by a society seeking truth. In fact, every time I hear a so called "hero" interviewed on television, the so called "hero" does not feel they did something heroic. They claim they did "what anyone would do in that situation." They feel lucky that people consider them a hero. In a no free will based society people will either consider themselves lucky or unlucky or somewhere in between on this spectrum. People will still feel slightly praiseworthy and slightly blameworthy (for practical and pragmatic reasons) but not to the degree we currently hold so dear to us as the fabric maintaining our entire society (emotional reasons). On a larger "free will" based insanity scale: Nations, religions, and groups of people cast severe free will based emotional blame onto one another all the time. Wars leading to more wars demonstrate that there has been very little to no progress in the understanding or acceptance of the concept that free will is total illusion and total utter nonsense. The Illusion of Free Will is a very bad and dangerous habit and an extremely hard one to break (kind of like smoking). For example: when a nation, religion, or a people decide that another nation, religion, or a people has a set of values that they don't agree with or like, the pervasive attitude is that it is much easier to bomb someone else's house (and assume they have free will) than to clean up one's own home (and get the illusion of free will thing right once and for all). The word Hero or Heroes is great for marketing purposes: For example: Heroes tend to "sacrifice." There is no such thing as sacrifice. A better word for sacrifice is investment. In fundamental reality—there are fundamentally no such things as heroes, sacrifices, martyrs, villains, and saints. Without free will—people are fundamentally neither praiseworthy nor blameworthy and cannot be held ultimately responsible or accountable for anything they do (or say). In practical, logistical, conventional, useful, surface, superficial reality there are in fact heroes and villains and everything in between. Here are some examples in practical reality: Yes you "sacrifice" for your children and spouse (which may or may not make them and you happy). Yes you "sacrifice" for your country or parents (which may or may not make them and you happy). Yes, you may martyr yourself for your country or cause (which may or may not make them and you happy). Yes, you may do "altruistic" charity work (which may or may not make them and you happy). These are all examples of pragmatic methods of how people attempt to make themselves and other people happy. Now for the fundamental (deepest truth) level. None of these examples, of course, really involve sacrifice, martyrdom, or altruism at all in fundamental (true) reality. What is really involved at its most basic and fundamental level is selfishness and personal investment for a better life somewhere down the road (delayed gratification). The person who is doing all this "sacrificing, martyring, and altruism" is fundamentally (truly/really) acting on the conditioned or instinctual belief that the good they hope to receive back from their efforts will be worth their time, energy, effort, money etc., in exchange for such things as God's good favor, good afterlife, having people like them, having people think they are a "good person" etc. They are not "sacrificing." They are selfishly investing (in/for a better life while alive or after life – getting into heaven for example).

People whether they admit it or not want a [1]*"perceived fair exchange of their human energy" that they had expended in the doing of all their good deeds for the other person(s) or cause(s). They want a return on their investment (time, effort, and energy). What about the person who risks his life to save another person? Again, we must understand the two levels of a no free will reality. On a useful/superficial/practical/pragmatic Level #1 of reality this person is in fact a hero. This person acted "selflessly" and did in fact "sacrifice" himself/herself: Being regarded as a Hero who did a great heroic sacrifice is a fantastic pragmatic and practical way to attain a tremendous amount of human energy (attention, special treatment, admiration, love, and sometimes even money). But on the deeper and truer/fundamental level – Level #2 – this person is fundamentally doing this: This person risked his life for another because he was acting on the belief that risking one's life in trying to rescue the other person will make this person feel better knowing he tried to save the other person than live the rest of his life with the thought/guilt that another human being died whom he might have otherwise been able to save. As you can see from the sentence above, there is no sacrifice and nothing heroic was done. This person acted selfishly in their own best interest so that they would not have to live out the rest of their life guilt stricken. To clarify above: What is the difference between "fundamentally and pragmatically?" Fundamentally means in the eyes of the Almighty/Creator. It is the deepest and truest nature of something. This is also known in some circles as "the absolute" or "the divine." Pragmatically means in the eyes of human beings (during the waking hours). It is on the most practical and superficial level of what is most useful. *See another example of the pragmatic level at the end/bottom of this insight/chapter. My advice to people who aren't sure if they have

---

[1]* Learn this concept in my book Enlightenment Through Entitlement by Nicolas Vale and The Celestine Prophecy: An Adventure by James Redfield

free will or not is this: Read this book and any other book you can find on the topic that argues against mankind having free will. Simply google the topic and buy the books. Then do the same for the books that argue that man does in fact possess a free will. Then lose interest in the topic or not (it's all fated anyway how much interest you have in this topic in the first place). Simply hear both sides of the story and then decide whether you believe you have it or not. To be fair to yourself and to the topic at hand, don't you believe you owe it to yourself to give equal time, effort, and energy to both sides?

Now for a quick change of topic:

Here's how you can quickly and easily refute anyone arguing with you about having free will: Ask the free will believer to give an example of a choice that they believe was freely chosen. Wait for their answer. Now ask the free will believer to say whether the choice was caused (what their reason/rationale was for the choice they made). Again, wait for that answer. Congratulations! You have just won the argument that everything must have a cause or reason/rationale. Then there is a cause to that cause, a cause to that cause, a cause to that cause, a cause to that cause, a cause to that cause, stretching back moment by moment all the way back before the free will believer was born.

Where is the free will?

Another reason free will is a myth.... Think about it, if human beings had free will all "choices" would be exactly 50/50. This means you would have no preference(s) for the desirability of any of the so-called choice(s). You would be frozen solid with indecision for all of eternity. It's only because we don't have free will that anything gets done at all.

* Defendant says, "I had no choice your honor."

Judge says "I also have no choice. For pragmatic reasons I have no choice but to keep society safe and you now need to be removed and reconditioned so that you will no longer make society unsafe."

The Celestine Prophecy Fulfilled: The Insight of No Free Will

The Greatest Gift

Yes, I know, not having free will kind of sucks because we cannot just choose to be happy whenever we want. Not having free will is also a really depressing bummer and very stressful knowing that we have no control over our own damn lives. So yes, not having free will does suck <u>BUT KNOWING WE DON'T HAVE A FREE WILL IS PARADISE</u>. There is a big difference between the two. The Greatest Gift of all is the knowing that our deepest truest self is truly, deeply, and fundamentally innocent – just like a perfect Angel.

We almost always (if not always) pursue what we perceive to be right and fair. If it means we must hold someone blamelessly responsible and <u>pragmatically</u> sue someone then that is what we must do. Now that we all know that free will is pure illusion, we just can't <u>fundamentally blame</u> people and banish their souls to an eternity burning in hell or put devil's horns on them with a red coat and a pitchfork. Actions will always have pragmatic consequences but will also always have fundamental innocence. The fundamental innocence of all of mankind is the greatest gift of all. If you must deeply, severely and fundamentally blame, then deeply, severely and fundamentally blame the situation (or the entirety of the universe), not the other person or yourself.

"You can still fear people. You just can't hate them."

—Sam Harris

"One Thing Leads to Another...then it's easy to believe somebody's been lying to me. One thing leads to another."

—One Thing Leads to Another song by The Fixx 1983

People don't like to take responsibility for their actions because deep down and fundamentally there was no other choice in the situation (with the data, knowledge, and consciousness they had at the time). People are always doing the very best they can. To be clear, everything in life (during waking hours) is a pragmatic attempt to attain a *perceived fair exchange of human energy (time, attention, labor, effort, money are forms of human energy). Due to the optimization imperative, we have no choice but to maximize and optimize every second of our life so that we can shield ourselves from the terrible emotion of regret and "if only I had done this and that differently." So, we have no choice but to always be doing the best we can (at the time!). Sometimes, if doing the "best we can at the time" means staying in bed all day then so be it. It may seem to others on the outside that we are being lazy, but due to all the invisible pressures, stressors, and causes we feel, sometimes we simply cannot get out of bed. Just staying alive sometimes is "doing the best we can" at that moment in time. Our bodies, for all sorts of emotional and physical reasons, simply cannot muster up the strength to get out of bed and do well anything. When we stay in bed all day and night, very little human energy is expended, and then very little human energy will be expected in.

---

* Learn this concept in my book Enlightenment Through Entitlement by Nicolas Vale and The Celestine Prophecy: An Adventure by James Redfield

The Greatest Gifts:

Once you realize that your decisions were all predetermined, and that you had no choice but to make them, you can immediately forgive yourself for all the silly and stupid mistakes that you made. That is the greatest gift of all. The other great gift in life is that since we do not have free will we cannot fundamentally rank destinies.

For practical reasons we like to, but fundamentally (truly) and ultimately, we cannot. We cannot compare our lives to others and rank or judge who has a superior or better life (thanks to no free will). As they say, "Compare and despair." The Messiah is not a person. The Messiah is the natural law that man's will is not free. By understanding that man's will is not free, people will in fact be saved from many highly toxic and self-destructive thoughts and behaviors. Believing in free will is totally, completely, and utterly nonsensical (not to mention insane). It is also a royal pain in the ass. Once you give up your belief in free will, you will release the heavy burden of comparing yourself to others. Who needs a belief that causes so much stress and agitation? This is because once we realize our karmic trajectories were not chosen freely by us, we have no choice but to not "compare and despair." How can we be upset with ourselves for not attaining or accomplishing more with our lives when our karmic streams were predetermined to begin with? Nothing is fundamentally our fault or our accomplishment – so now we can no longer rank human destinies. This gift is the realization that jealousy is an emotion based on humans having free wills. Since that premise is false, then jealousy is fundamentally a "false" emotion, or an emotion based on an illusion.

All people (including you of course) accomplish things or screw things up just because they or you were fated to do so. The universe compels you or them to do what you or they do. No one is acting with free will, so that should free you or them of arrogance or conceit, jealousy and destiny ranking. No one had, has, or will have a choice in the matter of anything. For example, I was simply fated to write this book, and you were not.

Deep down we know that we are always doing the best we can in any circumstance even though it may not appear that way to others. This is yet another reason that makes free will impossible. If we are always doing the very best we can then everything had to turn out exactly the way it did (and will). Everything can therefore be considered God's will. Deep down we know that we couldn't have done otherwise in every single situation we were ever in and will ever be in. For example, Elliot Rodger knew he was twisted. That's why he called his manifesto "My Twisted World." Therefore, this proves humans do not have free will. Why would someone who knew he was twisted not untwist himself? Surely step one is acknowledgement. The truth of the matter is …..he was just a witness to his own life. We all are. If he had free will, surely, he would have untwisted his "twisted world." He could not do otherwise because his will was not free. This is the one gift he left behind. He clearly showed in his detailed manifesto how man's will is not free (even though he thought he and others had it). He even said he "didn't want things to turn out this way." I think Elliot would have felt a whole lot better if he knew his will (and the will of others) was not free. He would have hated others far less for rejecting him. Yes of course, he would still have felt pragmatic mild disappointment and pragmatic mild sadness even if he knew the women had no choice but to reject him. That's just being a human being. But the (free will based mindset) emotion of deep seething hate (and subsequent desire for retribution) that he wrote about was falsely created by the false (and very harmful) belief in free will. There is no doubt about it that he assumed just about every single person he met (that had rejected him) had "freely willed" to reject him and that they could have easily done otherwise and accepted him (and hence not rejected him). This added an extra layer of rejection that is much more severe, intense and mean than a no free will based mindset rejection would have been. His free will assumption added a layer of nastiness, intent, meanness, and well **WILLFULLNESS.** It's like assuming someone is going out of their way to reject you when they don't have to. This is why the free will belief is so harmful. So, what is the solution? If we can constantly remind ourselves that our will (and the will of others) is not free, then destiny ranking, rejection, self—blame, other blame, self-hatred, other hatred, and all the mistakes we (and others) made in the past and will be made in the future can all be easily forgiven.

So, what is the Greatest Gift?

The Greatest Gift of No Free Will is saying this to yourself at a certain time of day. When is that? It's at Bedtime (the very end of your Waking/Competition Hours). See Insight 2 Bedtime (Level 2/Fundamental Level of the no free will reality)

"The greatest gift of all is the gift of unconditionally accepting yourself and others. The best way to achieve this goal is to understand man's will is not free. What a relief to know that I can say goodbye to all the silly mistakes I (and others) made in life. All I had to do was understand the illusion of free will. Once this understanding was internalized, I immediately forgave myself (and others) for everything that I felt I or they had done wrong in my life. I now know deep down and truly (fundamentally) that we all did the best we could at the time and that everything was and will be predetermined. I remind myself of this truth each night just before I go to bed."

The Celestine Prophecy Fulfilled: The Insight of No Free Will

Reviewing The Two Levels of Reality

This concept is so vital it's worth reviewing (from Insight Two). Evolution can be scary. Evolution might not be understood and may be poorly judged. But, to evolve is to change to better oneself and to always be open to new ideas. The major thrust of The Celestine Prophecy now being fulfilled is to establish at long last that free will is pure illusion and that this realization is what the 1993 Celestine Prophecy prophesied would occur (a breakthrough in spirituality was about to occur is what The Celestine Prophecy foretold). In the grand scheme of things, thirty plus years is a very short period. Different times call for different minds. Just like we once all thought the world was flat or that the earth was the center of the solar system, we must now all come to a point collectively and realize that free will is a grand hoax, a grand illusion, and a grand myth. Quite simply stated, mankind has been duped. One of the most important implications of a no free will world reality, is to understand the difference between the **<u>fundamental reality/level</u>** of your life and the **<u>pragmatic reality/level</u>** of your life. There is a huge difference between the fundamental and the pragmatic, and understanding this difference is job number one if you are to fully understand and internalize the teachings of this book. This is why we review it again and again. Free will believers make no distinction between the pragmatic and the fundamental levels of reality as they believe people are truly to blame or praise for their actions and it's all just one reality. Non free will believers now know better because they have read this book and now know that the pragmatic/superficial/surface level of reality attributes/imbues people with blameless or faultless responsibility/accountability (so called pragmatic "blame") while the fundamental reality attributes/imbues people with total and complete innocence and does not hold people responsible or accountable for anything.

Once again, The 2 Levels of the new No Free Will Reality.

The (Waking/Competition Hours) Pragmatic/Practical/Useful Reality – Level #1. This level is necessary to correct our behavior (and others) and so that we can penalize, reprimand, admonish, and if necessary, sue people to hold them pragmatically (blamelessly) responsible and/or (blamelessly) accountable (including financially of course as money is a form of human energy). This is a fake/pretend (tip of the iceberg) reality in a way, but it is a useful reality especially since human beings have no choice but to battle and play the game for human energy. For the time being (it's going to be a good long while I'm sorry to say), you may consider this reality the "act as if" you have free will even though you know you don't have it level/layer/tier to reality. The reason why I say for the time being is because eventually when the entire world understands that free will is an illusion, "acting as if" you have free will will come across as being just plain silly. But you must know (and I am sure you will agree) we are many decades away from this happening. Therefore, "for the time being" most likely means many decades if not centuries. This battle for human energy (that we have no choice but to compete for) is well discussed in The Celestine Prophecy: An Adventure by James Redfield (1993 book) and subsequent 2006 movie of same name. I also discuss this concept in length and in detail in my book Enlightenment Through Entitlement by Nicolas Vale published in 2004.

The Fundamental/Truest/Deepest Reality – Level #2 (Bedtime/no more competition) – This level is the spiritually awakened and enlightened level of ultimate truth. This level to reality is the deepest and truest. This is also known in some circles as "the absolute" or "the divine." On this level we see that mankind is fundamentally totally and completely innocent for absolutely everything. No one is responsible or accountable for anything on this level. This is because we know deep down that free will is an illusion and doesn't exist.

Some Definitions:

Pragmatic means how human beings may aspire to act or behave, but not as they believe to be true deep in their hearts. What is the most economical way to be in terms of time, effort, and energy? What is the easiest thing to do versus what is the truth of the matter? What is the pragmatic nature of a human being?

Pragmatic Synonyms: Sensible, businesslike, commonsensical, down-to-earth, efficient, logical, matter of fact, practical, reasonable, hardheaded, mundane, no-nonsense, plainspoken, useful, what gives the most utility, the shallow and superficial/surface level of something.

Fundamental means what human beings believe to be true deep in their hearts and what their core essence is. What is their true nature and what can they not help but do?

Fundamental Synonyms: Basically, centrally, essentially, inevitably, certainly, accordingly, as a matter of course, automatically, axiomatically, by its own nature, cardinally, compulsorily, alone as such, by and of itself, by definition, by its very nature, by itself, fundamentally, in essence in itself, the deepest and truest level of something.

Let's continue now…

The question of whether we have "free will" has been hiding in academic circles and philosophy classes for thousands and thousands of years. It is now time to take this matter straight to the heart and center of Main Street on Truth Avenue. The people now need to know the truth. The truth is this: **<u>Man Does Not Have Free Will.</u>**

Life is predetermined and is just a matter of fate. Nothing is up to us, and we are just along for the ride.

You either have free will or you don't. Many people love to tell me "I have a little free will." I need to report to you the following: There is not an in between or grey area. You either have it or you don't. There is no "I have a little free will."

It's a black or white issue.

So here is a quick snapshot of how society will improve once The Insight of No Free Will (Celestine Prophecy Fulfilled) has been completely fulfilled and implemented.

| | | Note Level (pragmatic level) |
| FREE WILL | VS | NO FREE WILL |
		(fundamental level)
Human Emotions with Free Will 100% Positive we have Free Will and believe so does everyone else Model		Human Emotions without Free Will Know we have zero Free Will
Severe and Intense Anxiety (with Free Will)		Mild Concern (pragmatic)
Severe and Intense Depression (with Free Will)		Mild Sadness (pragmatic)
Severe and Intense Shame (with Free Will)		Mild Disappointment (pragmatic)
Severe and Intense Guilt (with Free Will)		Mild Remorse (pragmatic)
Severe and Intense Resentment (with Free Will)		Mild Resentment (pragmatic)
Severe and Intense Hurt (with Free Will)		Mild Sorrow (pragmatic)
Severe and Intense Anger (with Free Will)		Mild Anger (pragmatic)

Blameful Responsibility (with Free Will)	Blameless Responsibility (pragmatic)
Blameful Accountability (with Free Will)	Blameless Accountability (pragmatic)

Severe and Intense Jealousy (with Free Will)	Mild Jealousy (pragmatic)
Arrogance (with Free Will)	Humility (pragmatic)
Look what I did! I deserve a medal! (with Free Will)	I will accept the medal for pragmatic reasons. Reward is accepted to motivate others to do the same pragmatically. I accept the pragmatic praise. (pragmatic)
	By the Grace of God or compelled by the entirety of the universe = With gratitude. I am lucky. I don't deserve any praise. (fundamental)
What a terrible thing I did, I deserve to die! (with Free Will)	I will accept my punishment for pragmatic reasons and deter others from doing the same thing I did. I will accept being removed from society only to be rehabilitated and to deter others and keep society safe. I do not deserve to die. I accept blameless responsibility, and I am pragmatically to "blame." (pragmatic)
	My actions were compelled by Fate/Universe/God. I am fundamentally innocent. I don't deserve any blame/responsibility/accountability. (fundamental)
I'm a Hero (with Free Will)	I will accept the hero label for pragmatic reasons. God/Universe/Fate has cast me in the hero role. I will accept being called a so called "hero" to motivate others to do the same "heroic" thing I did for pragmatic reasons. Society needs to be motivated to pragmatically do "heroic" things and if idolizing me as a

	hero helps that to happen than its okay with me. I accept the pragmatic praise. (pragmatic)
	Timing intersected with good preparation - By the Grace of God or compelled by the entirety of the Universe. I am lucky. I am not a Hero. I don't deserve any praise. (fundamental)
I'm a Villain (with Free Will)	I will accept the villain label for pragmatic reasons. God/Universe/Fate cast me in the villain role. I will accept being called a "villain" or "evil" only to be "punished" pragmatically so that I deter others from acting the way I did for pragmatic reasons. I accept blameless responsibility. I am pragmatically a so called "villain" (pragmatic)
	Timing intersected with poor preparation. It is what it is. It was fated to happen and I'm curious to know why. I am fundamentally innocent. I am unlucky. I don't deserve any blame/responsibility/accountability. I was fated to be a villain or evil. (fundamental)

As you can see from above: One reality—the "free will" reality shows human emotions as "severe and intense." The other reality – the one without free will shows human emotions as milder and more muted: The world without "free will" has a much better chance of being a kinder, more gentle, placid, calmer and serene place. In conclusion, such things as religion, conventional morality, and the criminal justice system, at least as practiced today, owe much of their underpinning to an unexamined faith in a traditionally conceived free will model of society. How these current societal structures and institutions will change and evolve once The No Free Will Insight is widely accepted remains to be seen. In theory though, the reality of no free will (both levels pragmatic and fundamental) should bring about a kinder and more compassionate world.

There are two levels of reality in the world of no free will. #1 There is the superficial and surface <u>pragmatic level.</u> This is the level of pragmatic blameless/faultless responsibility and accountability. This is the level of you don't have to deeply or truly blame a flat tire (malfunctioning robot/human being) to fix it. Pragmatic blame is all you need. And #2 the <u>fundamental level.</u> The fundamental level is the deepest and truest level of reality. It is the level on which all human beings are exactly equal (like perfect angels) in their total and complete innocence. On this level no one is responsible or accountable for anything.

The Celestine Prophecy Fulfilled: The Insight of No Free Will

The Unconscious Also Proves No Free Will

Why am I writing this Insight/Chapter in this book? I really have no idea, but I know there must be a cause for it somewhere because everything has a cause. Whether or not it's unconscious or subconscious is just semantics and splitting hairs on what those two words mean. All I know is that I am not fully conscious or aware of what all the reasons and causes are to why I am writing this at this exact moment in time. Do I want to be understood? Do I want to make money? Do I want to be liked? Do I want to use this book to connect to people? Do I want to feel as though I accomplished something worthwhile? Do I want to seek the truth? Do I want people to respect me? Do I want to try and make a difference in the world? Is it all the above and then some? Probably but I'll never know for sure. The sub/unconscious mind (often simply called the unconscious) is all the processes of the mind which are not available to consciousness. The term unconscious mind was coined by the 18th century German romantic philosopher Friedrich Schelling and later introduced into English by the poet and essayist Samuel Taylor Coleridge. The concept gained prominence due to the influence of Austrian neurologist Sigmund Freud. Unconscious phenomena have been held to include repressed feelings, automatic skills, unacknowledged perceptions, thoughts, habits and automatic reactions, complexes, hidden phobias and desires. Within psychoanalysis, the cognitive processes of the unconscious are considered to manifest in dreams in a symbolic form. Thus, the unconscious mind can be seen as the source of dreams and automatic thoughts (those that appear without any apparent cause), the repository of forgotten memories (that may still be accessible to consciousness at some later time), and the locus of implicit knowledge (i.e. all the things that we have learned so well that we do them without thinking). In everyday speech and in popular writing, however, the term subconscious mind is often used interchangeably with the term unconscious mind. For the purposes of this insight/chapter, I will stick with the term unconscious to mean both the subconscious and unconscious. The unconscious mind can be thought of as a repository for socially unacceptable ideas, wishes or desires, traumatic memories, and painful emotions put out of the conscious mind by the mechanism of psychological repression. However, the contents do not necessarily have to be solely negative. In the psychoanalytic view, the unconscious is a force that can only be recognized by its effects. In other words, it expresses itself by the symptom(s) it creates. Unconscious thoughts are not directly accessible to ordinary introspection. They are supposed to be capable of being "tapped" and "interpreted" by special methods and techniques such as meditation, random association, dream analysis, and verbal slips commonly known as a Freudian slip, examined and conducted during psychoanalysis. What can I say about the unconscious other than the fact that we are not aware of what's in it – for it is unconscious. Unconsciously, subconsciously, semi—consciously, or consciously the universe compels people to pragmatically expect others to live up to their side of the bargain or keep up their end of the deal. "A deal is a deal" people often say. It appears that the pragmatic pursuit of a *perceived fair exchange of human energy is the default setting (during waking hours). Everyone can relate to the fact that we can only have one thought at a time. Therefore, every thought we have ever had and every feeling we have ever had gets relegated to this big storage center of all our experiences in the unconscious. People often do not know why they do what they do yet are driven to do

---

* learn this Celestine Prophecy concept in my book "Enlightenment Through Entitlement"

something. Most people do in fact have un/subconscious goals. Therefore, it is safe to say that many criminals who commit heinous acts of crimes and violence haven't a clue why they committed these terrible acts. They can guess what their true motives were, but they don't have a clue. We are only conscious (not conscious control, but more like a witness or simply just aware) of a tiny fraction of all the information we have ever received in life (tip of the iceberg). In fact, most of our life is in our un/subconscious. We cannot be conscious of our un/subconscious. Yes, we may have predispositions to certain moods if certain external events happen, but neither philosopher, theologian, neuro - scientist, nor physicist, will ever be able to fully explain why our brain states change the way they do. All we know at this point is that everything has a cause. It might be better to say it this way: "Everything has an unconscious cause." Each morning, I wake up and have two packets of oatmeal. Today I had three. I have no idea why. The main discovery of The Celestine Prophecy being fulfilled (insight of no free will) has a very clear claim about what is going on here. As you know by now, the fulfillment of the prophecy claims that human beings do not have free will. So then if humans are not the captains of their own ship, then what is? We can now assert with confidence that the unconscious (the unfree will) is always compelled by the universe to pragmatically attempt to receive back a *"perceived fair exchange" of human energy (one's attention, one's money, one's effort etc.) that was given to other people and other things/entities like nature and God. Is this correct? Who the hell knows? Sounds good to me, but if I'm only conscious of a tiny fraction of my life's history, there is no way to know for sure why I do anything. All we have left is a hypothesis or theory. The best guess scenario of why humans do what they pragmatically do (which is to chase greater life satisfaction

---

* learn this Celestine Prophecy concept in my book "Enlightenment Through Entitlement"

via perceived "fair" *exchanges of human energy) is the best we can do at this time. Perceived fairness gives us great satisfaction because there is no guilt and no resentment. We desire to get exactly what we feel entitled to.

Two examples of the unconscious in daily life: Every day when I leave for work, I take my cell phone with me. Last week I simply left without it. I have no idea why. I need my cell phone desperately each day for business reasons, yet I've noticed that about four times a year I simply leave home without it. The last twenty-seven years that I've owned a cell phone, I have noticed that there is a slight pattern—I simply forget my cell phone about four times a year. There is no rhyme or reason that I can think of as to why I do this, but I do. I simply walk out the door without it and I don't know why. If people, including myself, often have no idea why they do what they do, how can free will exist in the world? How can human beings have free will when the unconscious never sleeps and is often running the show? Do not underestimate the power of the unconscious in refuting free will. Freud popularized the idea many years ago that the unconscious was the captain of the ship, and it still stands true to this very day. The fact that the unconscious is in charge is yet another reason that makes free will impossible (like you needed another). People often "surprise themselves."

Another Example:

Just last month I was playing basketball. I play in a league that plays almost every week. I have been playing for about five years now. In these last five years I have averaged about six points per game. I focus mostly on good defense and rebounding. My outside shot is lousy, and I don't have any confidence in my inside game. I also have no idea how to drive the lane. I also play with guys who are

---

* learn this Celestine Prophecy concept in my book "Enlightenment Through Entitlement"

twenty years younger than I am, and I tire easily. I am often gasping for air while they are still at full speed. I know my game (so I thought) and play within my abilities. I know my role and play into my strengths and away from my weaknesses. I have only tried at most five "3 pointers" in the last five years and I made one of them. A month ago, I was unstoppable. I scored twenty-five points (by far my all-time high). I made four "3 pointers" out of six attempts. I was "unconscious." I was in some sort of "zone." After that game, I went back to scoring my usual six points (making layups after offensive rebounds). I have no idea what came over me that night I scored twenty-five. I slept just as well, ate just as well, and had the same type of day at work. What caused me to suddenly make twenty-five points? Is that "free will?" If that is—why can't I freely choose to do it again? I've played four more times since that game, and I can't seem to get more than four or six points no matter what I tell my mind to do. Why can't I just choose to do it again? The night I scored all those points something did in fact come over me and I felt out of control (and I didn't get tired either— which never happens). How can that be "free will" when I felt out of control? Is this how crimes and murders happen? Someone just snaps and gets out of control for no apparent reason. How can it be "free will" when I can't simply choose to do it again? Why was I so "out of character" that night? I don't know, will never know. If I knew, I'd obviously want to do it again . . . and again . . . and again. Something mysterious came over me. Maybe it was a full moon? Maybe I was hit by cosmic rays that day? Maybe the "stars were aligned" in a certain way (people sometimes actually say this)? Maybe it was a song I heard earlier that day? Maybe it was a song that was playing very softly in the gymnasium that I couldn't even consciously hear? I really have no idea what came over me. Many people have conscious goals. But then they "self-sabotage" themselves. Why would someone "self-sabotage" him/herself? Why would someone who works at a place where drinking on the job is forbidden get caught drinking on the job the day before he gets promoted (and hence lose the promotion)? His proclaimed and conscious goal (of five years mind you) was a promotion to manager. He had never drank alcohol previously while on the job in the last five years that he was employed there. Why the day before? What is going on here with self-sabotage? Just because you don't consciously know what the cause is, doesn't mean the cause doesn't exist. The cause exists and doesn't care if you are aware of it or not (for it's in the sub/unconscious). People mistakenly believe they have free will because they make what they believe to be uncaused choices or decisions. This gives people an **illusory feeling** of free will. The truth of the matter is that everything has a cause, and more often than not, that cause is in the sub/unconscious. There are causes in the environment that people are unaware of causing their decision making. For example, a certain type of music in a restaurant causes the patron to order a certain type of wine (from a certain country). When asked why they chose that wine, the customer will say "it tastes better."

People have sub/unconscious goals. I have no idea why this insight/chapter is ending now, but I'm sure there's a sub/unconscious cause or reason for it. Do not underestimate the sub/unconscious as a very convincing way to refute free will.

The Celestine Prophecy Fulfilled: The Insight of No Free Will

Why Free Will is Bad for Society

The Surprising Link Between Homicide Rates and the Belief in Free Will. New research suggests we believe that people have choices because we want to see some of them get punished.

A new study which was published in the Journal of Personality and Social Psychology shows in many ways how and why the belief in free will is bad for society. The hypothesis of the study as stated by the authors was to "propose that the pervasive belief in free will partially flows from a desire for moral responsibility to justify punishing others for their anti-social behaviors. Therefore, when there is a desire to punish, people should be motivated to believe in free will." In other words, people enjoy being on what one could call the "moral superiority thrill ride." This means that when people believe in free will, they also open the door to feeling morally superior to another. This is one of the many reasons people thoroughly enjoy their nonsensical belief in free will. When they see someone else do something wrong (the bad guy), and they believe that the wrongdoing was freely willed, it automatically makes the non-wrongdoing person (the good guy) feel better about themselves and in a sense morally superior. This is what makes people enjoy telling other people that a certain "person is crazy and evil and will spend the rest of eternity rotting in hell." It's a classic case of it makes me feel better to see someone else do something wrong because clearly, they could have used their free will and not done wrong. They made a bad free choice (free will) and they should suffer for this bad free choice (free will). Clearly, they could have done otherwise. A team of authors from several universities (the University of California-Irvine, Yale University, and two others) have put the above thesis to the experimental test.

The study then proceeds to back up its hypothesis in five separate experiments. In one of the experiments, 277 students in an undergraduate psychology course got a surprise email from their professor two days after they had taken their midterm exam. The email they received said one of three things: 1) that a student had been caught cheating on the exam, and had been punished; 2) that someone had cheated on the exam (because a cheat sheet was found in the exam room) but the perpetrator had not yet been identified or punished; or 3) that an un- described "activity" would be taking place in the next class (the "control" group).

Then, all the students were asked to complete a questionnaire asking their level of agreement with statements like "criminals are totally responsible for the bad things they do" and "strength of mind can always overcome the body's desires." Sure enough, the students who had read the emails about cheating (emails one or two) showed a stronger belief in the existence of free will than the students who had received the control email (email three). Three other experiments reported in the paper reached a similar conclusion using a variety of different designs and methodologies. Finally, to top it all off, the researchers conducted an independent analysis of real-world statistics that are relevant to the question at hand. The study authors proceeded to look for a relationship between a country's average belief in free will and homicide rates in that country, hypothesizing that more crime-ridden places would also tend to believe more strongly in free will, presumably out of a desire to see criminals punished. They were able to obtain adequate data for 74 countries. And sure enough, for these countries there was a marked relationship between homicide rates and belief in free will. For instance, countries like Venezuela, Columbia, and Guatemala—which have very high homicide rates (Venezuela's was about 45 homicides per 100,000 people in 2010) —also have citizens who believe strongly in free will. It is therefore safe to deduce that the following two societal problems are made worse by the belief in free will (and hence why free will is bad for society).

#1 That if the belief in free will is strongly present, people will be more likely to deeply, fundamentally, and truly blame another for their actions (as opposed to just pragmatically blame them for their actions). This feeling of deep hate towards another human being can only increase feelings of homicidal rage and seeking revenge (want to see another suffer and be punished). Deduction: More Homicides. Result - Bad for Society.

#2 Therefore, it also follows that the belief in free will is also responsible for deeply, fundamentally, and truly blaming oneself for one's actions. This feeling of deep hate towards oneself can only increase feelings of feeling like a failure, severe depression, severe regret, severe guilt, and suicidal urges/ideations (rage towards ourselves and want to see ourselves suffer and be punished). Deduction: More Suicides. Result - Bad for Society.

Here are nine more studies published in research journals that suggest attributing blame correlates with people having . . ..

*1 more aggression and violent seeking of revenge and retribution
*2 less forgiveness
*3 more interpersonal conflict
*4 less compassion
*5 less charity
*6 more anger towards others
*7 more anxiety and depression
*8 more arrogance and belittling of others
*9 more self -blame and guilt

*1 Folger and Baron, 1996; Wickens, Wiesenthal, Flora and Flett, 2011

*2 Bradfield and Aquino, 1999; Meneses and Greenberg, 2011

*3 Cashmore and Parkinson, 2011; DeBoard-Lucas, Fosco, Raynor, and Grych, 2010; Meneses and Greenberg

*4 Decety, Echols and Correll, 2010; Zucker and Weiner,1993

*5 Campbell, Carr and MacLachlan, 2001; Carr and MacLachlan, 1998; Cheung and Chan, 2000

*6 Csibi and Csibi, 2011; Decety, Echols and Correll; Martinko and Zellars, 1998; Meneses and Greenberg

*7 Csibi and Csibi; DeBoard-Lucas, Fosco, Raynor, and Grych; Fourie, Rauch, Morgan, Ellis, Jordaan and Thomas, 2011; O'Connor, Kotze and Wright, 2011; Raskauskas, 2010

*8 Decety, Echols and Correll; Miceli and Castelfranchi, 2011; O'Connor, Kotze and Wright.

*9 Csibi and Csibi; Fourie, Rauch, Morgan, Ellis, Jordaan and Thomas; de Guzman et.al., 2010 Nicolle, Bach, Frith and Dolan, 2011; O'Connor, Kotze and Wright

The evidence is clear: The stronger the belief in free will the more likely these two bad things for society will occur – Homicide and Suicide

Another reason why free will is bad for society: It's because free will is bullshit (Total BS). Bullshit is inconsiderate, deceptive, deceitful, hateful, merciless, unfriendly, unkind, uncompassionate, discourteous, disrespectful, cold, mean, inhumane and cruel. On the other hand, honesty is cordial, kind, loving, clean, courteous, respectful, truthful, compassionate, gentle, gracious, genuine, sincere, trustworthy, considerate and friendly. As we learned as children, honesty is the best policy. So, I ask you, – do you want to live on a kinder, truer and better planet? If so, then the above are just a few of the many reasons why understanding the honest truth that free will is an illusion is for the betterment of mankind.

The Celestine Prophecy Fulfilled: The Insight of No Free Will

Politicians, Philosophers, Scientists

For as long as I can remember, I was told "it's your choice." But is it? The answer may surprise you. My reality is that what I wanted to happen almost never happened and that a new belief system was needed to accommodate my reality that "do this to get that" never seemed to work. So, the surprising answer is this. You could not have done otherwise – so therefore, everything is predetermined. If you believe in Free Will then more self-awareness is needed. All you need to do is pay very close attention (self-awareness) to the cause and effect in your life and pay very close attention to you being you each day and how things get done (keep a journal if need be). As Sam Harris has said "What evidence could possibly be put forward to show that one could have acted differently in the past?" Free Will is false. Free will doesn't exist. Free will is an illusion. However, you word it — there is no such thing as free will. We must all come together now as a species and put all our different backgrounds aside. We must all unite in the most important discovery in the history of time and start discussing openly and honestly what it means that human beings do not have free will. This fascinating truth will change EVERYTHING as it makes it more obvious why a Universal Basic Income (UBI possibly by age) is simply the moral thing to do (the older you are the more UBI you get). Politicians like Bernie Sanders and Andrew Yang understand that gargantuan income inequality is immoral and wrong, but they never say why that is so. The reason why is because free will is an illusion and life is only about fate and luck. Everything must have a cause or reason, everything is conditioning, you could not have done otherwise, you have no choice but to choose what you feel is best for you to choose at the time with the data you have at the time, humans have a subconscious/unconscious, and you did not choose your parents or soul/spirit or how you were raised (nature and nurture). The world is either deterministic or indeterministic and neither grants free will. There is no third option. Why is this obvious truth being ignored or going unaddressed in the media? Let's change that! This hotly debated topic is now gaining daily momentum into the mainstream. If in fact free will is an illusion as many now claim it to be, the implications of this bombshell discovery will shatter how people go about their lives and will be talked about everywhere all the time for there is no more important topic as it touches everything we do as human beings. Thinkers have long recognized that free will – free choice, the ability to have done otherwise – is an illusion. As Darwin put it, "the general delusion about free will [is] obvious", or as Freud put it: "I am sorry to say I disagree with you categorically over this." Einstein stated that, "I do not at all believe in human freedom in the philosophical sense. Everyone acts not only under external compulsion but also in accordance with inner necessity." Not only does the non-existence of free will reduce to the evidence of neurobiology, but also reduces to a fundamental issue within logic. If we do in fact live in a deterministic universe, a universe of cause and effect, then we act as we do because of the biology we inherit and the environment we are raised within. Our character, our choices, would be the direct result of the pure luck of that biology and upbringing, and there would be no freedom of choice, no ability to have done otherwise. But even if we were subject to indeterministic effects (aka the quantum world of uncaused actions), there would also be no freedom of choice, because indeterminism means that our thoughts and actions would be of a perfectly random nature and would also emerge from outside of our conscious choice or control. Speaking of Quantum Mechanics – All the double slit experiment proved is that particles can behave probabilistically. Quantum physics/mechanics is based on probabilities. Probabilistic behavior does not grant free will. Probabilities arise from underlying causality. Let's hear what famous theoretical physicist Brian Greene has to say about this: Brian Greene (famous theoretical physicist) has said that quantum mechanics is a deterministic theory. What he means by this is that even though it only predicts probabilities for outcomes, the underlying laws governing quantum systems are strictly deterministic. This means that given a complete set of initial conditions, the theory will always predict the same probability distribution of possible outcomes: essentially, the probabilities themselves ***are determined*** by the quantum mechanical equations, not random chance. Gerard 't Hooft (Nobel Prize in Physics 1999) also believes that there should be a deterministic theory underlying quantum mechanics. What does this all mean in layman's terms? Let's look at a simplified example we can all relate to: Playing Craps in a Casino: What is the probability of rolling snake eyes? That's rolling a one with a one. The odds of that are $1/6 \times 1/6$ which equals one out of 36 times that event will occur. What determines how the dice roll is completely up to such causal things as the angle you roll the dice, how heavy the dice are, the speed and force you spin the dice, the weight of the paint dots on the face of the dice, the release point, the humidity in the air, how high the dice were thrown, how bouncy the surface is they bounce on etc. etc. The point is this - how the dice land (what number) is <u>completely caused</u> by many variables. It has nothing to do with free will. It has everything to do with causality. <u>Probabilities in Quantum Physics arise from underlying causality</u>.

Back to causality now:

Free will is not rescued by Quantum Physics/Mechanics. Deepak Chopra's "Quantum Consciousness" gives mankind free will is Quantum Bullshit. It's just the way rich guys like himself justify their high salaries and five star hotel lifestyles. As stated at the very beginning of this book, this quote below always seems to ring true (and that's why it's worth repeating):

"It Is Difficult to Get a Man to Understand Something When His Salary Depends Upon His Not Understanding It."

— Upton Sinclair

And all the Heisenberg Uncertainty Principle proved is that measurements cannot be precise enough when the scale becomes infinitesimally small and minute. This is why we cannot simultaneously precisely measure the position and momentum of a particle with perfect accuracy at the same time. The more precisely you measure one, the less precisely you can measure the other. This measurement impossibility has nothing to do with free will. So free will is not saved by these genius Quantum Physicists no matter how hard they try to convince you otherwise. Most Quantum Physicists/Spiritualists are so prejudiced and biased in favor of free will that they will twist and contort the results of almost any experiment in such a way that allows them to fraudulently claim there's free will. For example, Deepak Chopra - His answers are almost always misguided or misleading. Chopra misunderstands or misrepresents quantum physics to support his metaphysical "there is free will" claims (due to his motivated reasoning and wishful thinking to justify his high salary and five-star hotel lifestyle). But to be fair, we must always remember to give Chopra a bit of a break (due to the illusion of free will). Why is that? This guy has no choice but to try and earn a nice living like so many of us. He has no choice but to lack some integrity with his nonsense theories on why there is free will. So yes, we can pragmatically blame him, but we must be careful not to blame him too severely for he has no choice in the matter. His nonsense theories are part of his personal causal history, and he has no choice in the matter. It is his shtick and how he earns a living: Once again Upton Sinclair – "It Is Difficult to Get a Man to Understand Something When His Salary (good position/high standing in society) Depends Upon His Not Understanding It."

Are we to believe subatomic particles have free will or that they are caused? And just because we do not know how or why they are caused does not grant free will for human beings.

"Based on the current laws of physics, there's just no room for human intervention, no room for what we usually call 'free will.' We are all collections of particles that fully play by the rule of physics. There's no place we can step in and change the course of how hose particles – you and I evolve. The sensation of free will is real, of course. But that's all it is – a sensation."

—Brian Greene (Famous Theoretical Physicist)

"Quantum Mechanics as currently understood is deterministic. The strange feature is what it determines — the probability of what will happen."

—Brian Greene (Famous Theoretical Physicist)

Why is Free Will skepticism never uttered at our presidential debates? Is it because it seems to be so anti-freedom, so anti-American, and so politically incorrect. But at what cost? If we (USA) are the world leaders (or want to be in almost everything else), why can't the good old US of A be the leader in philosophical thought, intellectualism, and reality? We owe it to ourselves as a nation and more importantly as a species to get this right once and for all. Why shouldn't this question "do you believe in free will?" or more simply put "Is there free will?" be asked at our debates? The goal of civil discourse after all is to promote open and honest debate that is necessary to advance civil society in a meaningful way. If free will were debated, the current free will model of society would be criticized and deemed unfair. The current social inequality and so-called institutional racism would be called out as being exacerbated by the current free will belief system. The Horatio Algier myth would be illuminated. This myth is the idea that anyone can rise above their circumstances to achieve success through hard work and sound ethics. The myth of using your hard work and drive to make yourself a success sham/scam would be exposed once and for all. In short, criticism of the current free will belief (that society holds so dear) would be great because without it there is no progress. Now let's talk about something else which is to distinguish between a "cause" and a "reason." The truth is they are one and the same except a "cause" is usually meant to convey an actual physical cause. And a reason is usually referred to as an immaterial cause. Now here's the kicker… both (or either) must happen in <u>A MOMENT IN TIME</u>. Each domino (moment in time) is the <u>ENTIRE STATE OF THE UNIVERSE</u> which includes all Quantum Physics/Mechanics, all thoughts, all beliefs, <u>all reasons</u>, all intentions, all illusions, all magic and wizardry, all intuitions, all hunches, all desires, all supernatural activity, all psychic and paranormal phenomena, all occultism, all mysticism, all divine interventions if you believe in such a thing, all likes and dislikes, all Ghosts/Spirits/Souls, all Indeterminacy or Randomness Etc. – it includes everything and anything including all nothingness (if you believe in such a thing) in the universe – mental, emotional, spiritual, psychological, material and immaterial etc. etc.

EVERYTHING MATERIAL AND NONMATERIAL. But the point here is the word REASON. An example of a reason would be "I made that choice because I'm a good person." It's an abstract concept "I'm a good person" so people may say that proves free will exists because it's not a "physical cause" like for example someone knocking into you on the street and making you fall flat on your face. Don't think of reasons as immaterial causes and here's why – this is why they are in fact physical causes…. Now at what exact time did the reason occur (come into existence)? Let's say it came into existence on October 27th at exactly 323pm in the year 2024. So, once it happens (the reason) in a moment in time, it enters the physical universe. Remember time is a measurement and Einstein's general theory of relativity established time as a physical thing – it is part of space-time. Google it to learn more. So, to be clear, to refute free will you can just as easily substitute the word reason (so called immaterial/non-physical phenomena) with the word cause (so called material/physical phenomena). Just for the record, I do believe "reasons" also have physical neurobiology and brain states/chemistry attached to them but one need not believe this to be so to refute free will. One day, scientists will discover that all reasons/thoughts will have traceable physical evidence/brain states directly matching with them, but we are not at that point yet. So, it is clear, everything happens because of a CAUSE or REASON that preceded it (in a moment in time) and there is no escape no matter how hard you may try. In conclusion it does not matter if you use the word cause or reason when refuting free will with personal causal history learning curve chain theory. This is because a personal causal history chain of causes and/or reasons must happen in moments in time.

How big is this Fulfillment of The Celestine Prophecy? The prominent philosopher John Searle has said that were mankind to accept that free will is an illusion it "would be a bigger revolution in our thinking than Einstein, or Copernicus, or Newton, or Galileo, or Darwin." And this is probably not an overstatement by any stretch of the imagination. This is because free will skepticism is vastly unique in combining a gigantic intellectual realization that places man back firmly at the heart of the natural world with vast political, social, and cultural implications.

What must you do now?

One must open the door to the possibility that things are not what they seem to be – and if this is allowed, we should be able to expand our minds some to ultimately conclude the unflinching truth that free will is in fact an illusion. It is time now we all come together and see through this illusion of free will so that we can better and more accurately discuss what it means to be a human being living on planet earth.

If you don't agree with me that free will is an illusion, then a leap of faith is necessary for you at this time. All that is then needed within this leap of faith is just a small opening that comes from a small voice from inside your head that whispers, what if? What if free will is in fact an illusion? And from this small little seed and voice from deep within you, you might be surprised what will grow. At the very least you may learn something new, even if it is that which you refuse to believe, that which you reject. You will learn to understand that there is another side to this story that man has free will. Whether or not you end up agreeing with me that free will is an illusion, it remains true, nonetheless. Each person does perceive reality differently, but reality could not care less. There is a truth to reality. 2 + 2 = 4. People might perceive that 2 + 2 = 5, but it is their perception of reality that is incorrect. Reality does not fit your perception. It's the other way around as you try to match your perception to reality. It is time to shed some light on this truth about man's will not being free, on this truth which has been hidden. It is time to challenge the free will paradigm. Free will is a myth, free will is false, free will does not exist, free will is in fact an illusion. There is so much peer pressure to believe in free will that I am truly amazed to learn how many people don't believe in it. It is estimated that 10-15% of the world's population currently DOES NOT BELIEVE IN FREE WILL. These people for the most part remain silent and do not publicly tell others that they feel this way. It is not known why non-free will believers or free will skeptics are afraid to tell others that they feel this way, but it probably due to the fear of public ridicule and to avoid a heated argument. Here is the truth of the matter: Sinners are merely poorly programmed computers. They are not to blame because they weren't in charge of the programming. Any crime, no matter how heinous it was, can be traced back to the antecedent conditions acting through the accused's physiology, heredity, and environment. Crime = C. So, there's C-1, C-2, C-3, C-4, C-5, C-6, C-7 regressed all the way back to the beginning of time. The numbers just equal moments in time. We do not need free will to have morality. All we need to be moral is to be rewarded when we do good things and punished when we do bad things. Philosophy class and esoteric academic circles need to now come to the people with the truth about the illusion of free will. It is time now for the people to finally know the truth about their human wills not being free. Stop reading this book now. Close this book right now and sit quietly for 20 minutes and "freely will" one thought repeatedly. Freely will only one thought. Can you do that? If you have free you will be able to do that. Where is the free will? Why can't people keep their new year's resolutions? Where is the free will? We all know life is unpredictable. Unpredictability has nothing to do with rescuing the concept of free will. Just because you cannot predict something does not mean that it is not predetermined. There are too many variables to calculate. Does a hurricane have free will even though it is very unpredictable? Where is the free will? Why is quantum mechanics often used to try and salvage free will? Is it because such experiments like the double slit experiment are not predictable and are only based on probabilities? Again, unpredictability has nothing to do with rescuing the concept of free will. Just because you cannot predict something does not mean that it is not predetermined. Variables may be too numerous or too small to calculate accurately (such as The Heisenberg Uncertainty Principle). Furthermore, there could easily be hidden laws or hidden variables involved not yet discovered by humans. Where is the free will? Do subatomic particles have free will? I think not. They are either caused or random and neither can rescue free will. We can choose our desires, but we do not get to choose what our desires are in the first place. You are simply just lucky if you only have moral desires. You Could Not Have Done Otherwise. Period. Case Closed. No Free Will. Society has conditioned us to falsely believe that our wills are free. Law and order will not break down once everyone understands the illusion of free will. Actions will always still have consequences with or without free will. What will be left behind is the very *excessive* and *very deep* blaming. Free will is a myth of epic proportions and a huge monster secretly ruling our society. Whatever happens to us each day has been meant to have happened to us from the beginning of time. Events are either caused or not caused (random) or some combination of both. Either way, free will is impossible. All humans get programmed.

The program we are running is to seek pleasure and avoid pain. We have no choice but to follow and obey this programming. It is an immutable law of the Universe.

"There's not much downside to abandoning the notion of free will. It's impossible, anyway, to act as though we don't have it: <u>you'll pretend</u> to choose your New Year's resolutions, and the laws of physics will determine whether you keep them. And there are two upsides. The first is realizing the great wonder and mystery of our evolved brains, and contemplating the notion that things like consciousness, free choice, and even the idea of 'me' are but convincing illusions fashioned by natural selection. Further, by losing free will we gain empathy, for we realize that in the end all of us, whether Bernie Madoffs or Nelson Mandelas, are victims of circumstance — of the genes we're bequeathed and the environments we encounter. With that under our belts, we can go about building a kinder world."

— Jerry Coyne (Famous American Biologist)

*"We may regard the present state of the universe as the effect of its past and the cause of its future. An *intellect which at a certain moment would know all forces that set nature in motion, and all positions of all items of which nature is*

*composed, if this *intellect were also vast enough to submit these data to analysis , it would embrace in a single formula the movements of the greatest bodies of the universe and those of the tiniest atom; for such an *intellect nothing would be uncertain and the future just like the past would be present before its eyes.*

— Pierre Simon Laplace, *A Philosophical Essay on Probabilities*

*Laplace's demon is a hypothetical being that could predict the future if it knew the position and velocity of every particle in the universe at a given moment in time. The concept was proposed by French mathematician and scientist Pierre-Simon Laplace in 1814. Laplace's demon illustrates the idea of determinism, which is the belief that the universe is completely knowable, and the past completely determines the future. The demon's vast intelligence and infinite computational power would allow it to calculate the future of every person, planet, and particle.

"The mind is determined to wish for this or that by a cause, which has also been determined by another cause, and this again by another, and so on to infinity. This realization teaches us to hate no one, to despise no one, to mock no one, to be angry with no one, to envy no one."

— Baruch Spinoza (Famous Dutch Philosopher)

"For better or worse, dispelling the illusion of free will has political implications—because liberals and conservatives are not equally in thrall to it. Liberals tend to understand that a person can be lucky or unlucky in all matters relevant to his success. Conservatives, however, often make a religious fetish out of individualism. Many seem to have absolutely no

awareness of how fortunate one must be to succeed at anything in life, no matter how hard one works. One must be lucky to be able to work. One must be lucky to be intelligent, physically healthy, and not be bankrupted in middle age by the illness of a spouse. Consider the biography of a "self-made" man, and you will find that his success was entirely dependent on background conditions that he did not make and of which he was merely the beneficiary. There is not a person on earth who chose his genome, or the country of his birth, or the political and economic conditions that prevailed at the moment crucial to his progress. And yet, living in America, one gets the distinct sense that if certain conservatives were asked why they weren't born with club feet or orphaned before the age of five, they would not hesitate to take credit for these accomplishments. Even if you have struggled to make the most of what nature gave you, you must still admit that your ability and inclination to struggle is part of your inheritance. How much credit does a person deserve for not being lazy? None at all. Laziness, like diligence, is a neurological condition. Of course, conservatives are right to think that we must encourage people to work to the best of their abilities and discourage free riders wherever we can. And it is wise to hold people responsible for their actions when doing so influences their behavior and brings benefit to society. But this does not mean that we must be taken in by the illusion of free will. We need only acknowledge that efforts matter and that people can change. We do not change ourselves, precisely—because we have only ourselves with which to do the changing—but we continually influence, and are influenced by, the world around us and the world within us. It may seem paradoxical to hold people responsible for what happens in their corner of the universe, but once we break the spell of free will, we can do this precisely to the degree that it is useful. Where people can change, we can demand that they do so. Where change is impossible, or unresponsive to demands, we can chart some other course. In improving ourselves and society, we are working directly with the forces of nature, for there is nothing but nature itself to work with."

— Sam Harris in his book, *Free Will*

"Everything is determined ... by forces over which we have no control. It is determined for the insect as well as for the star. Human beings, vegetables, or cosmic dust - we all dance to the mysterious tune, intoned in the distance by an invisible piper."

— Albert Einstein

"Our actions should be based on the ever-present awareness that human beings in their thinking, feeling, and acting are not free but are just as causally bound as the stars in their motion."

— Albert Einstein

"Naturalistic evolution has clear consequences that Charles Darwin understood perfectly... [including the idea that] human free will is nonexistent...Free will is a disastrous and mean social myth."

— William Provine
Professor of History and Biology, Cornell University

"For me, the single most important question is how to construct a society that is just, safe, peaceful — all those good things — when people finally accept that there is no free will."

Determined: A Science of Life Without Free Will
— Robert Sapolsky Stanford Professor, Neuroscientist, Primatologist

The Celestine Prophecy Fulfilled: The Insight of No Free Will

Epilogue

The internet and cell phones have sped up growing up to such a degree that the problem of western societies in particular is that we no longer have to fight to just exist. We have more food than we need and warm shelter. Existence has become so easy that the only thing left to do on planet earth is to make the whole damn thing into a silly game. In other words, by making life into just a silly game, we can actually find some meaning and a reason to live. But what happens when the silly game becomes too stupid, boring, silly or difficult? Well then that's when our unfree will to live gets destroyed and suicide becomes a viable alternative to many of us. Why play a silly stupid game if we don't like it anymore? Then we invent new needs for ourselves such as stupid social constructs to stroke our egos with. These include such things as the "best" schools to go to, the "best" jobs, the "hottest" wife, the "best" country club to belong to, the "best" hotels to stay in etc. etc. I hate to say this, but that's all we have left. The need for love, a family, a perfect body, a car, a mansion, fame is really all pure stupidity if you really think about it. But that's all life is about now and it's understandable that many of us don't want to live on such a stupid planet—the "game" of life is quite ridiculous when all that is left is pleasing the ego. Then we must consider that even if we had eternal beauty, wealth and fame (or whatever else we so desired) we A) wouldn't appreciate it if we were born with it or B) would find earth even more bland and boring if we knew we always would have it. So, we're screwed either way because if we had all we desired forever and ever life would be even more boring, but on the other hand if we don't have it—then life becomes a silly and stupid game to attain such social constructs and ego pleasers. Admittedly, it is very hard or near impossible to penetrate through this sludge of social depravity since it has set in hard over the years. Prior generations have made it a way of life to want to "get ahead," and people have acquired the convenient skill of blocking off ideas, concepts, and suggestions that do not appeal to them (such as free will being an illusion). The shallowness of a "well adjusted" human being is downright frightful. If you were to point out the shallowness to a "well adjusted" human's existence, they would most likely tell you or snap at you "why are you so deep?" The ability to block pure logic (that man's will is not free) and consequently build a false or real happiness based on the current faulty model is simply not spiritually or fundamentally correct. Why is everyone living in the grand illusion that is free will? If everyone has it so wrong, then what is the answer to why we exist? The answer must be found in wanting to know the truth about things. You should not be hated, made to feel ashamed or guilty for any so-called psychological disorder (as long as you are not harming yourself or anyone else). This is true because everyone has his or her own unique and personal way to so-called "happiness" or a more peaceful state of mind. All you have to say to yourself is the following: "I know it's not everyone's path, but it is mine." I find all my beauty in this world in the truth that free will is an illusion. I prefer truths to lies every time because that's the only real beauty in this world that is left. Please just let me know the truth about things for it is the only truly meaningful endeavor that remains. That's all I ask. It's obviously not our fault, but The Universe has simply duped us all by this free will thing and it simply needs to be set straight once and for all. The time is now and that is crystal clear. Many of us who believe that free will is an illusion feel that no matter how many ways we phrase and rephrase what we are saying, we feel like we are talking to a brick wall. This is then usually followed by a weak sense of futility. Other times a strong sense of futility sets in. Either way a sense of futility sets in and then comes the "why does anything really matter?" feeling. The truth matters. It just does. Our species needs to get this free will thing corrected once and for all and for one reason and one reason only. It's simply the truth about reality. It's just not spiritually correct to believe in free will. What I am trying to say is that life for these newer generations seems to not matter much, if at all. The only possible way it could matter is to get to the truth of things since all other avenues to happiness now appear to be closed off. The last great truth to be discovered is that free will is just an illusion. This I feel will help mankind greatly as severe self-blame will soon cease to exist. When this begins to happen, people will in fact become a little happier. Take away free will, you take away severe self—blame. Once you take away severe self—blame, you basically instantly stop 99% of all suicides. This is because severe self—hatred or severe self—blame is simply not possible in a no-free will based mindset. What will remain in the no free will world will be the much saner pragmatic blameless responsibility/accountability mindset/perspective. Once people become armed with the knowledge that their messed-up lives were not and will not be their fault, people will start to once again begin to enjoy themselves. The pressure on all of us to have great lives will finally be off or even better the pressure we put on ourselves (or from our parents) to do so will be without the extra layer and weight of believing we are freely doing that to ourselves. We will now know the pressure is not self-inflicted or other-inflicted, but instead the demand(s) of a "great life" are coming from the entirety of the universe. Once you internalize the concept that free will is just an illusion, will you begin to truly smile again. This is because you will be living in the truth that none of this was your fault. Things and people just come here and exist the way they are and fated to be and that's just the way it is. As far as I can tell, the only real purpose of humanity is to now finally get this free will thing straightened out. The pursuit of truth is the only real purpose of being a human being. What else could it be? You see—you just can't lose once you understand that free will is just an illusion and that you are always doing the best you can.

There is always an "invisible gun to your head" as everything you do is the only thing you can be doing (or could have done) based on everything that has happened to you before. Yes, you are pragmatically responsible for your karma (cause and effect). But ultimately and fundamentally you are not responsible for your karma (cause and effect).

Neuroscience of free will refers to the recent neuro-scientific investigation of questions concerning free will. As it has become possible to study the living brain, researchers have begun to watch decision making processes at work. Relevant findings include the pioneering study by Benjamin Libet and its subsequent redesigns (Chun Siong Soon for example); these studies were able to detect activity related to a decision to move, and the activity appears to be **occurring briefly before people become conscious of it.**

If you contend that you are a "first causer" and a "little God" then you wouldn't know what to do next as every option would appear just as good as any other. You would magically lose all preferences and would no longer know what you preferred in any given situation . . . somehow all your past experiences would magically be erased. Choices are never 50/50—hence no free will. How could a free will believer prove there's free will? In theory only one way (as previously mentioned at very end of Insight Five). They would need a time machine/recorder and go back in time (rewind the tape of the universe). Press Play. Then see if everything turned out the exact same way or not. If it turned out differently then Free Will is proven, but if everything turned out the same exact way then there is no free will. The Celestine Prophecy being fulfilled declares that everything will always turn out the exact same way every single time.

We must always remember the following 4 things:

#1 We are lucky to have moral desires and unlucky to have immoral desires.

#2 Without free will, life just becomes a matter of luck or unluck. Luck or unluck means you cannot control it. It just happens and you have no control over how lucky or unlucky your time on earth feels to you.

#3 The belief in "Free will" is total and complete utter nonsense.

#4 Some people like to say what you "could have done." This is total nonsense since without free will there is no way to have done otherwise.

Once again as Sam Harris put it "What evidence could possibly be put forward to show that one could have acted differently in the past?"

Some other of my favorite Sam Harris quotes:

"Our wills are simply not of our own making. Thoughts and intentions emerge from background causes which we are unaware and over which we exert no conscious control. We do not have the freedom we think we have."

— Sam Harris

"What will my next mental state be? I do not know—it just happens. Where is the freedom in that?"

— Sam Harris

"How much credit does a person deserve for not being lazy? None. Laziness, like diligence, is a neurological condition."

— Sam Harris

"You are not controlling the storm, and you are not lost in it. You are the storm."

— Sam Harris

The Celestine Prophecy Fulfilled: The Insight of No Free Will

Summary of Why Free Will Is Impossible

You have no choice but to choose what you predict will give you the most amount of overall life satisfaction available to you at the time. You have no choice but to always go towards (seek) pleasure and away from (avoid) pain (doing what gives you the most amount of overall satisfaction). Yes, feeling depressed is the most amount of satisfaction available to you at the time. There must be some sort of satisfaction in being depressed unbeknownst to you (sub/unconscious). It is most likely to learn a life lesson that you need to learn. It is the lesser of two evils (or more). In short, depression and misery are not free choices. These negative emotions occur because your personal causal history learning curves require your depression, suffering, and misery to recondition you for future decision making. If you don't want to feel depressed at all then simply "snap out of it" and simply use your free will to get out of it. This is of course impossible. This is why most people must face depression and other negative emotions. They have no free choice in the matter. Surely, if people had free will, depression would not exist. We cannot stop ourselves from being born. We had no choice in the matter. We then have two choices. Commit suicide or live out our lives as best we can. Every moment in time, every motion, from the beating heart to the slightest reflex action, from all the inner and outer movements of the body, indicates that life is never satisfied or content to remain in one identical position for always like an inanimate object, which position shall be termed death. The present moment in time is (here) and the next moment in time is (there). Going to the spot (there) from (here) always has two options. You are now reading this sentence in a moment in time (here) and here are your two options: One can either remain living (there) or kill yourself (there). Either move to the next spot called (there) alive or move to the next spot called (there) dead (commit suicide). Consequently, the motion of all life is any motion from (here) to (there) – one moment in time to the next moment in time, is always a motion which you have no control over and hence man's will is not free. Every motion of life has no choice but to go in one direction and one direction only. This is the direction of greater satisfaction otherwise known as always being forced to attempt to attain more pleasure and therefore less pain. This is called The Pleasure Principle or seeking pleasure and avoiding pain (and obviously considering the ramifications of immediate vs delayed gratification or satisfaction or fulfillment etc. etc.). Since the motion of life always constantly moves from (here) to (there), which is an expression of dissatisfaction with the present position, it must naturally follow in the direction of greater satisfaction. It should now be obvious that our desire to keep living, to move off the spot of this moment (here), to the next moment (there) is determined by a masturbatory psychological law over which we have no control. We must always seek out more pleasure and greater overall satisfaction. It is therefore axiomatically impossible to purposely go towards less satisfaction. Even if we should kill ourselves in this very next moment (there), we are choosing what we believe will give us greater satisfaction, otherwise we would not kill ourselves. The truth is at any moment in time the motion of man's will is not free because his will must obey this natural and immutable law of the universe. Man is compelled by his nature to make choices that he prefers within the options available to him that will lead him under his present belief system to find greater overall life satisfaction. He must always choose what he believes will be better for himself and his overall set of circumstances (all things considered). Sometimes we endure short term pain for longer term overall greater life satisfaction (such as running a Marathon). There is no choice in the matter. Just by staying alive and not committing suicide, mankind has always been attempting to go in the direction of greater pleasure and overall life satisfaction. For example, when mankind found that a discovery like the automobile was for his benefit in comparison to travel by horse, he was compelled to prefer it for his transportation. The Amish people have no free choice but to still prefer horse travel because it gives them _greater overall life satisfaction_. This is what feels best to them psychologically based on their culture and belief system. It is patently axiomatically impossible to knowingly go in the direction of greater life dissatisfaction. If you are at this present moment in time (this exact instant) coming up with reasons why I am so wrong about this point (maybe even shouting at this book), then you are in fact in this very moment in time proving me correct. You are in fact obeying this psychological and natural law of the universe. By trying to prove me all wrong, you are by no will of your own trying to find greater overall life satisfaction. Maybe you will even write your own book about what The Celestine Prophecy being fulfilled means to you and how and why I am so wrong about free will being an illusion. You want to prove your point so badly and have no choice in the matter because it would give you greater satisfaction to prove me all wrong otherwise commit suicide. If suicide is less preferable currently (which I sincerely hope), then you have no choice (as long as you are staying alive) to prove me all wrong or agree with me (you have no choice but to do whatever gives you the most overall life satisfaction). So, since I am quite sure that of the three options, suicide will give you the least amount of overall life satisfaction, you then have these two remaining options: 1) Prove me all wrong or 2) agree with me. If you agree with everything I am writing here, then this is the option by default giving you the most satisfaction. Perhaps you will help join the No Free Will movement and pass this book along? Consequently, during every moment of man's existence (progress) he always did what he had to do because he had no choice. This no choice is to always go towards greater overall life satisfaction based on one's best estimation and prediction of what would bring him or her the most overall life satisfaction. Regardless of how many examples you experiment with, the results will always be the same because this is an immutable psychological and natural law. You simply cannot purposely choose what gives you less satisfaction. You can choose your preferences, but you cannot choose _what you_ prefer in the first place. Your preferences are based on your genetics and conditioning. Free will is nowhere to be found. From moment to moment all through life man can never move in the direction of dissatisfaction on purpose, and that his every motion, conscious or unconscious, is a natural effort to get rid of some dissatisfaction or move to some greater satisfaction. It is now quite possible that my repetitiveness is making you less satisfied than you were before when my concept was new and fresh to you. Everything you do is a lesser of two evils (or the least of many evils). You simply pick or choose the best possible option which you predict will give you the most overall life satisfaction available to you at the time (from the viable options). This then becomes by default what you want to do (you have now chosen your preference/desire). Choice is determined (caused) by desire. You choose your desire and then do what you desire to do (from a list of possibilities). This is why man rarely, if ever, does anything "against his will." The only real way to do anything "against one's will" is to be tied up and brought somewhere (or left in a place tied up) or forced to do or say something with a proverbial "gun to one's head." In other words, made or coerced to do or say something otherwise face death, bodily harm, loss of money, or some other negative consequence. So even though man rarely, if ever, does something against his will (desire), this does not mean man's will is free. Hence, the confusion. The truth is man cannot choose what his preferences are to begin with. Preferences come from background causes for which man is completely unaware, exerts no conscious control of, and was not the originator of. One last reason on how we know free will doesn't exist – If I had a free will The Fulfillment of The Celestine Prophecy (this book) would have been perfectly written, been perfectly edited, been perfectly articulated, been perfectly presented, been perfectly organized, and not been so damn repetitive and redundant.

BOOK SUMMARY IS HERE

Summary Part One:
1. If Determinism is true, then there is no free will.
2. *If Indeterminism (true randomness) is true, then there is no free will.
3. Either determinism is true, or *indeterminism (true randomness) is true or some combination of both is true.
4. Therefore, there is no free will (from 1-3).

Summary Part Two:
The Two Levels/Layers of The No Free Will Insight into reality:

Waking/Competition Hours Level 1 – Free will is not needed to keep society safe. This is because a no free will society can exist and function very well in a pragmatic and useful way. A society of "pragmatic blame" aka blameless/faultless responsibility/accountability. This is the <u>pragmatic and useful superficial/surface level</u> of the no free will world (which keeps society safe). You do not need to deeply or severely blame (attribute free will to) flat tires/broken down cars/dangerous wild animals or people/malfunctioning robots to fix them/remove them. Pragmatic and useful blame is all you need. People/dangerous animals and things are pragmatically and blamelessly removed to keep society safe. People have no choice but to pragmatically and usefully (and don't forget blamelessly and faultlessly) seek pleasure and avoid pain and this includes wanting perceived fair exchanges of human energy in all their affairs. Please read the 1993 edition of The Celestine

---

* For the record I do not believe in indeterminism. Quantum mechanics is completely causal. Probabilities arise from underlying causality.

Prophecy and/or my book called Enlightenment Through Entitlement to learn more about the concept of human energy exchange and what is exactly meant by it.

Bedtime/Level 2 – Here we have the deeper, truer, and the <u>fundamental level</u> of the no free will world. This means there is no heaven or hell (no judgment day). Level 2 teaches us that all human beings are equally fundamentally innocent – just like perfect angels. Nobody deserves any deep or true or ultimate "the buck stops here" or "just deserts" fundamental blame or praise. Life is all luck or unluck and everything is fated (predetermined).

Summary Part Three:
There is no escape from the natural law of having no choice but to <u>seek</u> more and more overall life satisfaction. However, during our searching/seeking we often have no choice but to experience unpleasant emotions which we have no control over. These unpleasant emotions then become part of our personal causal history learning curve and recondition us. Everything is predetermined as we are always doing the best we can with the data and consciousness we had at the time.

Summary Part Four:
Free will justifies such things as poverty. This is why most wealthy people are very keen to keep this belief. These are the people who believe that all positions in life are somehow deserved. This is why it is very rare to find someone who has a good position in life (like Sam Harris) who comes out against the belief in free will. In general, the old adage of "never expect someone to understand something whose salary depends on them not understanding it" always seems to ring true.

Summary Part Five:
Why is understanding that free will is an illusion important? To list a few the belief in free will breeds and amplifies the following misconceptions, misperceptions, and highly toxic ways of being in the world: deep and excessive self-blame, deep and excessive blame of others, egoism, the illusion of deservingness over others, deep and excessive anger or hatred of others, divisiveness, allowance of inequality, poverty dismissal, fat shaming, gay bashing, desire for retribution or vengeance, non-connectedness, and the belief that some people are going to heaven while others will rot in hell for the rest of eternity.

Summary Part Six:
People often say "why bother" to change anything if everything is predetermined. Understanding that free will is an illusion does not give a person license to do whatever they desire. It doesn't give people an excuse to act on bad or socially unacceptable behavior. It also does not give a person the defeatist attitude of "why bother." In a no free will world, free will is an illusion but consequences of actions or inactions are still real. Causes or reasons will always trump everything. Therefore, there will always be reasons or causes for good lawful behavior and reasons or causes to "bother" (this is why we "bother" to look both ways before we cross the road). Reasons and causes come about causally just like everything else in life. The causes and reasons are always the same – we have no choice but to seek pleasure and avoid pain. This is why the people (such as me) who claim everything is predetermined and that there is nothing we can do to change that still "bother" to look both ways before we cross the road. We have no choice but to attempt to avoid harm and look both ways. There is a cause or reason for looking both ways which is our uncontrollable desire to not want to be hit by a car when we cross the road. In short, "bothering" to look both ways before we cross the road is also predetermined as we have no choice in the matter.

Summary Part Seven:

Do you get to choose your thoughts? If you could choose your thoughts certainly you would choose only happy thoughts.

No Free Will - Easy as 1-2-3

1. You act and think the way you do because of who you are (all things considered).
2. You do not get to freely choose who you are (soul/spirit and consciousness included).
3. Therefore, no free will.

"Man can do what he wills, but he cannot will what he wills."

— Arthur Schopenhauer (Famous German Philosopher)

Summary Part Eight:

To sum up, an event (aka "event causation") can either be caused or not caused. If it's not caused, then clearly you are not the cause of it and hence that specific event cannot be attributed to you or your free will. If the event is caused, you can be the cause (aka "agent causation") of that specific event, but not freely so. Why is that? #1 We are not first causers or little Gods. We obviously did not give birth to ourselves. We are not causa sui (the cause of ourselves or self-caused). We were born into and are part of a linear (past to present to future one moment in time and at a time) personal causal history learning curve chain of cause-and-effect conditioning. #2 Law of Causation …. There is always A WHY (cause/reason) as to why we make the "choices" we do and that (cause/reason) is to make the best "choice/decision" we can for ourselves at the time (we have no choice but to go in the direction of seeking greater and greater overall life satisfaction). Therefore, we can conclude, any combination of caused or uncaused event or agent causation cannot grant free will.

Summary Part Nine:
It is easy to conclude that libertarian free will is impossible and is false. Go back in time to any so called "free choice" you made with the exact same starting conditions. Other than causa sui and agent causation which are both false (see above in summary part eight), the only other conceivable way you could have done otherwise would be if you had <u>wanted to do</u> otherwise at the exact same moment the so called "free choice" was made. But since you <u>didn't want to do</u> otherwise (because of who you were at the time in totality and this includes your brain state obviously), you couldn't have done otherwise. This is very good news for you. Why is that? You no longer have to feel like a failure if you fail at something. That's because if you could have done otherwise, rest assured you would have done otherwise. As for "compatibilist free will" (meaning determinism and free will are compatible) nothing could be further from the truth. First, free will is a completely made-up thing and is not compatible with anything (because it does not exist in the first place). Second, it is especially not compatible with determinism as the very word determinism literally means that all events in the universe, including human decisions and actions, are causally inevitable (cause and effect). Therefore, we can conclude there is no such thing as "libertarian free will" or "compatibilist free will." In fact, there is no such thing as any kind of free will as it is an entirely made-up thing that people desperately want to believe is true. Wanting something to be true does not make it true.

Summary Part Ten:
"Investigators are looking for the cause to the fire." "What was the cause of death?" We often seek explanations for human behavior. When we seek to explain human behavior, we are seeking the reasons or causes for the behavior. This endeavor assumes determinism is true as we assume there must always be a reason for the behavior. Then there is a reason for that reason and a reason for that reason so on and so forth stretching back to before we were born. Where is the free will?

ABOUT THE AUTHOR

Nick Vale has a BBA from Emory University, an MBA in Finance from Fordham University, and is a proud member of Mensa (top 2% IQ society). He is a regular person and truth seeker. He feels that not being a professional philosopher, scientist, politician, or religious/spiritual leader is to his advantage as most of these experts are biased in favor of free will as they all suffer from motivated reasoning, cognitive dissonance, and wishful thinking. They cannot see the truth of no free will because they cannot be neutral or objective in this matter. The reason why they cannot admit the truth that free will is false is because doing so could-would-can-will cause them great harm (psychological/emotional and even financial). This quote below always seems to ring true for almost any successful person in any industry or profession. This is why I keep repeating it.

"It Is Difficult to Get a Man to Understand Something When His Salary Depends Upon His Not Understanding It." — Upton Sinclair

Other books you may like by Nick Vale are Enlightenment Through Entitlement (2004), Free Will Sam Harris (Sam Harris was Right 366 reasons why Free Will is an Illusion Everyday Calendar Book) (2017), The Holy Bible: No Free Will (2023). His websites are celestineprophecyfulfilled.com, nofreewill.org and nofreewill.info. To learn more, Google Holy Bible No Free Will Book Trailer by Nick Vale and Nick Vale interview with Logan Crawford on Spotlight.

The Celestine Prophecy Fulfilled: The Insight of No Free Will

REFUTATIONS OF FREE WILL

1. You Couldn't Have Done Otherwise.

2. You were/are always doing the best you can at the time.

3. Cause and Effect (Causality). There is only one personal causal history learning curve chain.

4. Who would be depressed or angry if they had free will?

5. You could have been born someone else and had such things as their morality, vices, bad habits, physiology, physical limitations, consciousness, intuitions, hunches, mind, spirit, and soul. You would be them (no ultimate moral responsibility).

6. If God knows everything, free will is impossible.

7. Free Will implies choices are exactly 50/50 and that we have no preferences.

8. We cannot decide outside of Nature and Nurture.

9. We have a subconscious/unconscious.

10. We did not self – cause ourselves (we are not first causers). We did not create ourselves and therefore are part of a causal chain of events.

11. Quantum Indeterminacy or true randomness does not give us free will.

12. Either Determinism or Indeterminism is true and neither gives us free will.

13. Pleasure Principle (we have no choice but to always attempt to seek pleasure and avoid pain). We have no choice but to try and attempt to acquire greater and greater overall life satisfaction.

14. Life is unpredictable. Unpredictability does not equal free will. Just because you cannot predict something does not mean it is not predetermined. There are too many variables to calculate (like a Hurricane).

15. We do not get to choose such things as our spirit, soul, personality, sensitivities, intelligence, or our consciousness.

16. If we had free will, who would freely choose evil? Why not freely choose to be a perfect angel all the time?

17. We can choose our preferences, but we cannot choose *what we prefer* in the first place.

18. We can choose our desires, but we cannot choose *what we desire* in the first place,

19. We can choose our wants, but we cannot choose *what we want* in the first place.

20. We cannot control or choose if or when we will be ready to change our mind about anything which obviously includes whether human beings have free will.

Benefits of No Free Will

- More Love Thy Neighbor as Thyself

- More Humility

- More Kindness

- More Forgiveness

- More Compassion

- More Gratitude

- More Understanding

- More Cooperation

- Less Self — Blame

- Less Other — Blame

- Less Self — Hatred

- Less Other Hatred

- Less Depression

- Less Anger

- Less Shame

- Less Embarrassment

- Less Anxiety

- Less Guilt

- Less Resentment

- Less Hurt

- Less Feeling Badly About Yourself If You Did Something Stupid or Wrong

- Less Feeling Like A Failure If You Fail At Something

- Less Jealousy

- Less Belittling Of Others

- Less Arrogance

- Less Aggression

- Less Violence

- Less Homicide

- Less Suicide

- Less Revenge and Retribution

*Law and Order (and morality) will not break down with the advent of the knowledge contained in this book. Actions will always still have *pragmatic consequences.*

**See bottom/very end of Insight/Chapter 7 - The Myth of Free Will*

Many things we accept today as fact were ridiculed and opposed to in the not-so-distant past; this goes to show that just because an idea is currently unpopular does not mean it won't be unilaterally accepted in the future.

Please pass this book to another person if you understand why showing the world that free will doesn't exist will be the biggest thing ever to evolve the consciousness of our species. If you for some reason cannot appreciate the importance of this work, then I will not blame you for your will is not free.

"History is not just the evolution of technology; it is the evolution of thought."

— James Redfield, *The Celestine Prophecy*

Now that we are done with this book. What does the term "Free Will"
mean to you?
What is your definition of it? Do you believe you have "free will?"
Now compare your notes here with those you made at the beginning
of this book.

THOU SHALL NOT FUNDAMENTALLY BLAME OR PRAISE

The Celestine Prophecy Fulfilled: The Insight of No Free Will

www.ingramcontent.com/pod-product-compliance
Lightning Source LLC
Chambersburg PA
CBHW022101050726
47591CB00002B/616